# Hunting in Eastern Han Tombs

Joseph M. James

Abstract

iv

During the first and second centuries CE colonists living along the Northern Frontier of the Han Empire built tombs with stone doorways that depicted scenes of the hunt. These reliefs depict a fabulous world inhabited by mounted archers, hybrid *xian* (immortals) and frolicking/fleeing animals. Within these reliefs there is also a limited tendency to draw on the alternate lifestyles of the Xiongnu, a confederation of northern nomadic tribes who served as both neighbor and foe to the Han Chinese who lived in this area. Previous scholarship has seen hunting imagery in these reliefs as passive reflections of the mixed culture and economy of the region. I instead maintain that it was part of an iconographical program that depicted and facilitated the passage of the deceased to paradise across the dangerous borderlands between Heaven and Earth.

My dissertation argues that imagery in Shaanxi and Shanxi was actually a refinement of earlier Eastern Zhou (771-221 BCE) and Western Han (206BC- 8CE) depictions of the hunt and immortals, but that in this region, the positioning of the hunt at doorways created a liminal space representing the "Great Boundary" between this world and the next. This world is described in an inscription from a tomb excavated in Suide, Shaanxi that warns the deceased of the dangers that confront him if he does not return to the world of the living. On the basis of this inscription and similar "soul-summoning" passages from the *Chu ci* (*Songs of the South*) and Eastern Han dynasty tomb-quelling texts (*zhenmu wen*), I argue that hunting imagery in Shaanxi and Shanxi belongs to the desolate spaces that were believed to exist between this world and the next.

iv

Furthermore, I conclude that these images were a local response adopted by the patrons because they lived in a militarized, colonized setting in which fears of foreign neighbors fused with their apprehensions of the 'beyond'.

TABLE OF CONTENTS

# LIST OF TABLES

# ACKNOWLEDGEMENTS

Numerous persons have been instrumental in bringing this work to completion. First and foremost is Professor Katheryn Linduff who throughout my academic years in Pittsburgh has been a constant source of inspiration, support and encouragement. I am also deeply indebted to the members of my committee, Professors Anthony Barbieri-Low, Karen Gerhart and Anne Weis, whose critical comments and intriguing questions have motivated and informed all stages of my research. All have spent a great deal of time editing and discussing my work; any errors or omissions in this thesis are my own.

I am also grateful for my colleagues and friends, Maria D'Anniballe, Shalmit Bejarano, Naoko Gunji, Han Jiayao and Yuki Morishima who have encouraged me throughout my graduate career. To Sheri Lullo and Rachel McTernan, I owe special thanks for asking critical questions that helped frame my research. My gratitude also extends to Zhang Haihui of the East Asian Library at the University of Pittsburgh for her help with my research and the translation of difficult texts. I would also like to thank Linda Hicks for the many cups of coffee and warm conversation that have enriched my graduate experience.

I was able to complete this research thanks to two Foreign Language and Area Studies (FLAS) Fellowships (Asian Studies Center, University of Pittsburgh), the China Studies Tuition Remission Scholarship (Asian Studies Center, University of Pittsburgh) and the Arts and Science

Fellowship (University of Pittsburgh). My travel to Shaanxi and Shanxi was also graciously supported by the John H. Tsui Memorial Award (Nationality Rooms Scholarship, University of Pittsburgh) and the China Council Pre-Dissertation Grant (Asian Studies Center, University of Pittsburgh). I would like to thank the faculty and staff of the Asian Studies Center at the University of Pittsburgh for their continued support, interest in my research and confidence in my work.

Finally, I would like to extend my thanks to my family and my husband for their love and support; this dissertation is dedicated to them.

## 1.0    INTRODUCTION

In the late decades of the first century CE, Chinese civil and military officials and wealthy individuals began to commission tombs in the northern portion of the modern province of Shaanxi. During the Eastern Han dynasty (25-220 CE) this area would have fallen under the jurisdiction of Shang and Xihe commanderies. Originally developed and colonized during the Qin (221-206 BCE) and Western Han (206 BCE-8 CE) dynasties, these commanderies served as a safeguard against the encroachment of the expanding Xiongnu Empire, a confederation of nomadic pastoralists that would remain the largest real and perceived threat to the Han Empire throughout its four hundred year history. Tombs in northern Shaanxi date from about 90 to 140 CE, a turbulent time period whose end is marked by the Han government's final loss of control in the region. At this time the capital, as well as the remnants of the government bureaucracy of Xihe commandery, moved east into modern Shanxi where tombs continued to be constructed until around 175 CE.

Tombs constructed in Shaanxi and Shanxi during the Eastern Han dynasty are noted for their elaborately decorated exterior and interior stone doorways; the walls and ceilings of the tombs being made of undecorated brick. The iconography of these doorways, most often carved in deep or shallow relief, include a number of different motifs many of which can also be found in the other areas of tomb production (Shandong, Nanyang, Henan, and Sichuan) during the first and second centuries CE. Reliefs from Shaanxi and Shanxi, however, rarely depict Confucian themes and instead frequently include motifs associated with immortality and scenes of the hunt. Hybrid *xian* (immortals), the goddess Xiwangmu, stylized versions of Mount Kunlun and other motifs of immortality show a clear interest by the patrons of these images in the immortal paradise of Xiwangmu. Beside such imagery tomb lintels in the region are decorated with scenes of the hunt that focus on the figure of the mounted archer, often turned in his saddle shooting behind him in the so-called "Parthian Shot."

Tomb reliefs from Shaanxi and Shanxi remain an understudied area in scholarship relating to Eastern Han tomb reliefs and it was not until fairly recently that scholars have even begun to take note of the immortality-centered nature of their iconography. The hunting scenes, however, have been discussed in previous scholarship alongside scenes of grazing and other images of "daily life." These types of representations have often been studied as a group and seen as characteristic of the imagery of tomb reliefs from the region. Regardless of the fact that these grazing scenes and so-called "daily life" scenes are not as pervasive as scenes of the hunt, all have been perceived as reflecting the mixed culture and economy of the region. Also often viewed as a symbol of status of the deceased, hunting scenes have always been seen as representing an activity that the deceased took part of while living and as separate and unrelated to the otherworldly imagery of hybrid-winged immortals and Xiwangmu.

General scholarship examining depictions of the hunt in Eastern Han tombs has also discussed images of the hunt as a homogenous category depicting images from life and representing either: 1) an activity that the deceased enjoyed in life and, through its depiction in the tomb, could continue to enjoy in the afterlife, or as 2) a reference to sacrifices made to the ancestors during the annual *La* festival, since the hunt was a major component of ancestral sacrifice and the word *lie* (to hunt) was pronounced almost identically to the word *la*. Although both interpretations are likely to be correct in certain contexts, they do not address and cannot explain the strongly regional character of Eastern Han hunting scenes, nor the reasons why such imagery would be combined with motifs of immortality in tomb reliefs from Shaanxi and Shanxi.

Rather than seeing these scenes as passive reflections of the real or desired life of their patrons, this study examines the significance of hunting imagery to mortuary traditions within the region. Based on their frequent pairing with motifs of immortality as well as the multivalent nature of the hunt in pre-Han and Han visual and textual traditions, I argue that hunting imagery in these tombs depicted the route through the desolate spaces that were believed to exist between this world and the next. Described in an inscription from Suide, Shaanxi, as well as in the *Chu ci* (*Songs of the South*) and *zhenmu wen* (tomb-quelling texts), these dangerous borderlands were believed to be inhabited by noxious spirits and wild animals waiting to harm the deceased at every turn. In order to arrive at the paradise of Xiwangmu that is depicted in tombs throughout the region, the deceased needed to pass through this dangerous realm. My dissertation argues that both hunting imagery and motifs of immortality in Shaanxi and Shanxi were placed in tombs to facilitate this process.

Fundamental to my study is the understanding of images of the hunt in this region as equivalent to things and actions that they depicted. More than simply reflections of the lifestyles of their patrons, I argue that scenes of the hunt were depicted in tombs in Shaanxi and Shanxi because they were believed to become the events and activities that they represented. As such, the hunt, through the act of subjugating and killing wild animals, was seen as fundamental to the passage of the deceased across the borderlands between Heaven and Earth.

I also maintain that this regional view of the afterlife and its emphasis on the hunt was the result of the turbulent and multi-cultural setting in which these reliefs were produced. Hunting imagery throughout the region focuses on the figure of the mounted archer. I argue that this figure was intended both to combat the malevolent spirits and wild animals that haunted the netherworld, and the Xiongnu themselves. Although the Xiongnu were probably both friend and foe to the patrons of these images, I suggest that in hunting imagery from Shaanxi and Shanxi, Han dynasty fears and perceptions of the world of both the Xiongnu and the Xionngu themselves fused with the idea of a wilderness populated by dangerous and alien creatures through which the deceased must pass.

Throughout this study I utilize a number of visual and textual sources to investigte my reading of this imagery. First and foremost I base my interpretions upon comparisons of scenes of the hunt in Shaanxi and Shanxi with other depictions of the hunt in pre-Han and Han China as well as their relationship with other imagery that decorates these tombs. My understanding of scenes of the hunt from Shaanxi and Shanxi is also based upon passages from received historical, ritual and encyclopedic texts as well as texts recently recovered from pre-Han and Han tombs. Although the received texts tend to be generalizing, making their application to local settings problematic, I maintain that they corroborate both the visual mortuary tradition depicted in these reliefs and the few inscriptions that have been found in tombs from Shaanxi and Shanxi.

In order to foreground these reliefs and their unique iconography, Chapter 1 provides a comprehensive survey of the archaeological and historical context in which the reliefs from Shaanxi and Shanxi were produced. It provides an overview of the general characteristics of tombs and tomb reliefs in the region as well as a history of their excavation and scholarship. In Chapter 1 I also survey the development of Shang and Xihe commanderies from their beginnings in the Warring States Period (475-221 BCE) to their tumultuous existence during the Han dynasty. Based on inscriptions from these tombs and received texts, Chapter 1 provides the most comprehensive survey of the history of these commanderies now avaliabe providing a picture of what life was like for the patrons of these images living along the Northern Frontier.

Chapter 2 details the distribution and characteristics of hunting imagery in each of the four main regions of tomb relief production during the Eastern Han dynasty demonstrating the unique nature and consistency of hunting scenes from Shaanxi and Shanxi. An analysis of this imagery by region shows that hunting iconography during the Eastern Han was far from homogenous. It also reveals one of the major shortcomings of previous scholarship that tends to lump imagery into one large category, regardless of content and distribution. Chapter 2 includes a discussion of this scholarship and its generalized interpretations of hunting imagery that argue they are reflections of the social status of the deceased or of contemporary life. I instead argue that in Shaanxi and Shanxi such imagery was part of a regional mortuary tradition and formed an active part of the process of the deceased's journey from the tomb through the borderlands between Heaven and Earth and finally to paradise.

The unique iconography of scenes of the hunt in Shaanxi and Shanxi along with its significance is examined in Chapters 3 and 4. My analysis of this imagery is grounded in Han and pre-Han visual traditions of the hunt as well as historical and ritual texts that address the importance of the hunt in ancient China. In Chapter 3, I investigate the relationship between hunting scenes and motifs of immortality in the decoration of tomb doorways throughout the region. Concentrating on compositions that include hunting scenes and images of immortals cavorting with birds and beasts, I maintain that hunting scenes from this area drew upon and expanded the relationship between hunting, exorcism and ancestral sacrifice expressed in earlier visual and textual traditions. I argue that the pacification of animals in both types of scenes signifies the exorcism of the borderlands between Heaven and Earth, either through the transformation of the ferocious animals in these reliefs into spirit-guides/helpers or through their death or capture.

Finally in Chapter 4, I focus on the motif of the mounted archer and other elements within hunting scenes that are associated in Han visual and textual traditions with the Xiongnu. I argue that the tumultuous and multi-cultural setting in which these reliefs were produced engendered a conception of the beyond flavored by the presence of the Xiongnu and other nomadic peoples. Although this imagery seems to forge connections between the borderlands between Heaven and Earth and the world of the Xiongnu as it is depicted in Han accounts, I conclude that in this imagery the Xiongnu were perceived of as being both capable of either thwarting or aiding the deceased in their journey to paradise.

**2.0    AN ARCHAEOLOGICAL AND HISTORICAL SURVEY OF EASTERN HAN**

**TOMBS FROM SHAANXI AND SHANXI**

Beginning in the late decades of the first century CE, Chinese civil and military officials and wealthy individuals began to commission tombs in modern Shaanxi with elaborately carved stone doorways. Although the construction of decorated tombs came to a halt in Shaanxi around 140 CE, similar tombs continued to be constructed in the east in Shanxi until around 175 when the Han government lost control of the region. Compared to other major regional production centers of Eastern Han tomb reliefs (Shandong-Jiangsu, Nanyang, Luoyang, Henan and Sichuan), the story of the patrons, images and the circumstances of tomb production in Shaanxi-Shanxi remains understudied in Chinese and Western literature. This chapter serves as the most comprehensive examination of these materials available in English and provides the archaeological and historical context in which hunting scenes from the Northwest were made.

The first half of this chapter consists of an overview of the history of excavation of Eastern Han tombs in the Northwest and reviews previous scholarship. This is followed by a summary of the different types of tombs excavated, the placement of reliefs within these tombs and the general artistic characteristics of tomb reliefs in the region.

In the second half of this chapter I focus on the history of the Han settlements in the Northwest, offering first an outline of their genesis, development and decline. I then concentrate on what life was like along the Northern Frontier. Using the standard histories, tomb inscriptions and tomb reliefs, I examine Eastern Han patterns of settlement and the prosperous and precarious nature of life in this region. The evidence suggests that the patrons of these reliefs were civil or military officials or private civilians closely associated with the military who lived in Han settlements where non-Han Chinese were the majority. As I will argue in what follows, this unique situation had a direct impact on the popularity and kind of hunting scenes that appear in these tombs.


## 2.1    HISTORY OF EXCAVATION AND SCHOLARSHIP


In Shaanxi, Eastern Han tombs have been excavated in the north in the Shanbei area. The majority of these finds are concentrated in the counties of Suide and Mizhi along the Wuding River (a tributary of the Yellow River).  Tombs have also been discovered to the far north in Yulin, to the east on the edge of the Yellow River at Shenmu, and to the west in Qingjian, Zizhou and Hengshan. Tombs in the Shanbei area date from about 90 CE to 140 CE; this final date marks the end of Han control of the area.  At this time the capital of Xihe commandery was moved to the east into modern Shanxi where decorated tombs continued to be constructed until around 175 CE. In Shanxi, Eastern Han tombs have been excavated in the Jinxi area around Lishi, to the south in Zhongyang and to the west in Liulin. Both Shanbei and Jinxi are part of a larger mountainous region in Northern China that lies on the edge of the loess plain and borders the desert and Inner Mongolia.[1]

---

[1] Xin Lixiang and Jiang Yingju, "Shaanxi, Shanxi Han huaxiang shi zongshu (A Summary of Han Dynasty Tomb Reliefs from Shaanxi and Shanxi)," In *Zhongguo huaxiang shi quanji*

Before the middle of the twentieth century little was known about the style, content or distribution of tomb reliefs from the Northwest. Eastern Han tomb reliefs were first recovered in Shanxi in 1919 with the discovery of the tomb of the Han official Zuo Biao (d. 150 CE) at Mamaozhuang, Lishi. After their discovery some reliefs were sold to buyers outside of China and today these stones remain in the collections of the Royal Ontario Museum.[2] Around 1920 several tombs were also found in Shaanxi and their reliefs were published in *Yilin yuekan* (*Art Forest, A Monthly Publication*). Nevertheless, the placement of these reliefs within their respective tombs and the area in which they were found remains unclear.[3]

After 1950, the scientific excavation, research and analysis of Eastern Han tomb reliefs can be divided into three periods. The first period begins in the early 1950s when based on the first scientific excavations in the Shanbei area scholars began to understand the distribution and characteristics of tomb reliefs in the Northwest. The majority of these tombs and their reliefs were discovered around Suide, Mizhi and Yulin. In 1959, the first major publication on tomb reliefs from this region, *Shanbei Dong Han huaxiang shike xuanji* (*Selected Carvings of Eastern Han Dynasty Tomb Reliefs from Shanbei*) was published that included reproductions of 157 reliefs, archaeological reports and scholarly analysis of the stones.[4] This publication was followed by several articles by Shih Hsio-yen that remain among the few resources in English that discuss Eastern Han reliefs from Shaanxi and Shanxi. Reliefs excavated in Shaanxi before

---

(*Collected Works of Chinese Tomb Reliefs*), Vol. 5 (Jinan: Shandong meishu chubanshe, 2000), 1-2.

[2] See Klaas Ruitenbeek, *Chinese Shadows: Stone Reliefs, Rubbings, and Related Works of Art from the Han Dynasty (206 BC-220 AD) in the Royal Ontario Museum* (Ontario: Royal Ontario Museum, 2002).

[3] Xin Lixiang and Jiang Yingju, 4.

[4] Ibid., 5.

1964 were also published along with those from other areas in a German publication by Käte Finterbusch in 1971.[5]

A second phase of research began in the 1970s with the discovery of more Eastern Han tombs outside the core sites of Suide and Mizhi in the Shanbei region. At this time Eastern Han tombs were also discovered in Shanxi especially around the Mamaozhuang site where reliefs from the tomb of Zuo Biao were first discovered in 1919.[6] The majority of reliefs from Shanbei and Jinxi excavated before the early 1990's were published in a compilation by Li Lin, Kang Lanying and Zhao Liguang, *Shanbei Handai huaxiang shi* (*Han Dynasty Tomb Reliefs from Shanbei*), in 1995.

By the third phase of research which began in early 1990s, archaeological excavations, research and analysis had described the styles, content and distribution of tomb reliefs in the Northwest. The 1990s marked the beginning of a second wave of discoveries, the most famous of which were the excavations of a Han dynasty city and accompanying tombs at Dabaodang, Shenmu, Shaanxi. Analysis of reliefs from this site confirmed and highlighted the use of under drawings, stencils and colored pigments in the creation of tomb reliefs in the Shanbei area. The early part of the present decade saw the publication of the archaeological report of Dabaodang (2001), a compilation of tomb reliefs from Suide (2001) and a volume of *Zhongguo huaxiang shi quanji* (*Collected Works of Chinese Tomb Reliefs*) (2000) dedicated to tomb reliefs from Shaanxi

---

[5] Käte Finsterbusch, *Verzeichnis und Motivindex der Han-Darstellungen* (Wiesbaden: Otto Harrassowitz, 1971); Shih, Hsio-yen, "Han Stone Tomb Reliefs from Shensi Province," *Archives of Asian Art* 14 (1960), 49-64; "Early Chinese Pictorial Style: From the Later Han to the Six Dynasties," (PhD Dissertation: Brywn Mawr College, 1961); "Some Fragments from a Han Tomb in the Northwestern Relief Style," *Artibus Asiae*, Vol. 25, No. 2/3 (1962), 149-162.
[6] Xin Lixiang and Jiang Yingju, 5.

and Shanxi. The introduction to this volume written by Xin Lixiang and Jiang Yingju is the most

comprehensive study of tomb reliefs from the Northwest.[7]

Apart from these compilations and the archaeological reports of the tombs themselves,

scholarship that concentrates on reliefs from the Northwest has been slow to develop. Before the

1990s these reliefs were ignored or relegated to the position of a footnote in literature that

focused on Eastern Han tomb reliefs.[8] This is especially true in English-language scholarship.

Although Shih Hsio-yen first introduced tomb reliefs from the Northwest in the early 1960s, only

two other works in English have since focused on these reliefs. The first of these, by Li Jian

categorizes and dates the carving style of reliefs from the region.[9] A second study, published by

Klaas Ruitenbeek defines the stylistic and iconographic characteristics of tomb reliefs from the

Northwest by focusing on a group of tombs excavated near Lishi, Shanxi.[10] Ruitenbeek's work

---

[7] Another detailed overview of tombs from the Shanbei region can be found in Wang Jianzhong, *Handai huaxiang shi tonglun* (*A Discussion of Han Dynasty Tomb Reliefs*) (Beijing: Zijin cheng chubanshe, 2001), 216-230. The strength of Wang's work lies in his division of the tombs in the Shanbei area into a number of categories based mainly on tomb construction, but Xin and Jiang's work is a more comprehensive study and discusses tombs from both Shaanxi and Shanxi.

[8] Exceptions to this general trend prior to the mid-1990s include Wang Yujin, "Cong Han huaxiang shi kan Sichuan, Shandong, Shanbei de Handai nongye (A Look at Han Dynasty Agriculture from Han Dynasty Tomb Reliefs from Sichuan, Shandong and Shanbei), " *Nandu xuetan* 1990(5), 10-14 and Kang Lanying, "Huaxiang shi suo fanying de Shang jun liehou huodong (Hunting Activities in Shang Commandery as Reflected in Tomb Reliefs)," *Wenbo* 1986(3), 48-52. Of course both articles focus on hunting and agriculture, themes that are often studied together as reflecting the daily life of the region and considered characteristic of tomb reliefs from the Northwest. The predominance of hunting scenes in the region is easily established, but agricultural scenes are not as prevalent as has been emphasized in Chinese scholarship.

[9] Li Jian, "Classification of Han Pictorial Stone Carvings from Northern Shaanxi," In *Eternal China: Splendors from the First Dynasties*, edited by Li Jian (Dayton, Ohio: Dayton Art Institute, with the cooperation of the Administrative Bureau of Museums and Archaeological Data of Shaanxi Province, People's Republic of China, 1998), 41-55.

[10] Klaas Ruitenbeek, "The Northwestern Style of Eastern Han Pictorial Stone Engravings: The Tomb of Zuo Biao and Other Eastern Han Tombs Near Lishi, Shanxi Province," *In Rethinking*

illustrates the type of scholarship that is needed in the study of these tomb reliefs. The second wave of discoveries in the region in the 1990s has also been followed by articles in Chinese that for the first time have taken the Shanbei and/or Jinxi tombs as their main focus of study. As of yet, however, no single work has fully explored the significance of the iconography of these reliefs or their relationship to the other main areas of relief production during the Eastern Han dynasty. By focusing on the theme of the hunt in the Northwest, this dissertation serves as the most comprehensive study of tombs in the region and addresses a major lacuna in the study of the construction of Eastern Han tombs and their reliefs.

The lack of scholarship prior to the mid-1990s that focused on tomb reliefs from the Northwest is the result of several factors: the geographic remoteness of the region, the relatively recent discovery of these tombs and the subject matter and appearance of the reliefs themselves. In the PRC, the Shanbei and Jinxi areas are still relatively underdeveloped and since archaeological discovery in modern China often goes hand and hand with economic development, until the last twenty years the flow of archaeological discoveries in the region has progressed at a relatively slow pace. The division of the Shanbei and Jinxi areas into separate provinces in the PRC has also meant that reliefs from this region have often not been studied as a unit, even though the later stones from Shanxi are clearly related to those from Shaanxi in both style and content. The comparatively slow rate of discoveries or research on the region has also meant that some of the most basic information about these reliefs was not accessible until recently. This includes their wide geographic spread (1970s) and the full extent of artisans' use of stencils and colored pigments (1990s). The status of this area as a frontier region during the

---

*Recarving: Ideals, Practices, and Problems of the "Wu Family Shrines" and Han China*, edited by Naomi Noble Richard (Princeton: Princeton University Press, 2008), 132-159.

Eastern Han dynasty also makes a highly-developed reconstruction of its history and the lives of the patrons of these reliefs more difficult than those that were created in the more populated (and peaceful) areas of the Han Empire.

Complicating matters is the fact that in many of these reliefs details were added using black or red ink and colored pigments, the result being that their visual richness is literally lost to the modern viewer. This, combined with their overall lack of Confucian themes, has meant that they have been considered by some to be the work of inferior provincial artists and/or lack intellectual interest.[11] Rather than focusing on Confucian themes, Northwestern iconography centers upon the ascension of the soul to the land of immortality, a process and belief that is not extensively discussed in Han texts. As such these tombs provide a valuable record of Han beliefs about the afterlife. Thankfully more recent scholarship has begun to recognize this as a distinctive and meaningful characteristic of tomb reliefs from Shaanxi and Shanxi.[12] This dissertation builds upon this scholarship by focusing on scenes of the hunt from this region, orienting them within the larger visual vocabulary of Han and pre-Han China and examining how they can contribute to our understanding of Han mortuary traditions.

---

[11] Li Jian, 43.

[12] See Hu Jie, "Shanbei Donghan huaxiang shi mu mumen quyu shen yi tuxiang hanyi zhi kaobian-- yigai diqu huaxiang shi mu mumen buwei shang chuxian de ruo gan zhongyao zhenyi ticai zuowei lunshu de zhongxin (Connotation Discrimination of Gods Portrayed in Stone Tomb of the Eastern Han Dynasty—Taking Important Subjects about Gods and Spirits in Tomb Door of Northern Shaanxi as a Narrative Centre)," *Yishu tansuo*, Vol. 20, No. 2 (April 2006), 5-16 and *Zhejiang yishu zhiye xueyuan xuebao*, Vol. 4, No. 3 (September 2006), 90-104; Sun Zhouyong, "Shanbei Han huaxiang shi shenhua ticai (Mythological Themes on Han Dynasty Tomb Reliefs from Shanbei)," *Kaogu yu wenwu* 1999(5), 72-78; Xin Lixiang and Jiang Yingju, 8-10.

## 2.2    TOMB CONSTRUCTION: GENERAL TYPES AND THE PLACEMENT OF RELIEFS WITHIN THE TOMB

All of the reliefs excavated from Shanbei and Jinxi decorate tombs; no above ground shrines such as those found in Shandong have been excavated in the Northwest. Although there are many variations, tombs in this region are basically either single or double-chambered; both types often have a small space just beyond the tomb door that one enters before proceeding toward the front chamber. A few tombs also have a small brick side chamber that is outside of the tomb proper just before the tomb doorway. Single-chambered tombs are relatively small in the region measuring around 4x2 meters and have barrel-vaulted ceilings (*quan ding*).[13]

The basic plan of a double-chambered tomb in the Northwest consists of a pair of rooms lined up front to back. The front room of a double-chambered tomb usually has a domed ceiling (*qionglong ding*) that is made of brick, while many of the back rooms have barrel-vaulted ceilings. The entire length of these two rooms is usually around 7 meters. Sometimes, as in the case of several tombs from Dabaodang, Shenmu, Shaanxi, the rear room lies off the central axis to the side of the front chamber. In the most complicated double-chambered tombs, additional one or two barrel-vaulted side chambers are attached to the left and/or right sides of the front room.[14]

---

[13] Xin Lixiang and Jiang Yingju, 5. For an overview of tomb types in the Jinxi region see Klaas Ruitenbeek, "The Northwestern Style of Eastern Han Pictorial Stone Engravings: The Tomb of Zuo Biao and Other Eastern Han Tombs Near Lishi, Shanxi Province." See Wang Jianzhong for further variations on the themes outlined here, 216-230.

[14] Wang Jianzhong, 220-221; Xin Lixiang and Jiang Yingju, 5. See Shaanxi sheng kaogu yanjiusuo and Yulin shi wenwu guanli weiyuan hui, eds, *Shenmu Dabaodang: Handai cheng zhi yu muzang kaogu baogao* (*Shenmu Dabaodang: An Archeological Report of the Remains of a Han Dynasty City and Tombs*) (Beijing: Kexue chubanshe, 2001) for diagrams of the tombs excavated in Shenmu representative of these trends.

A unique aspect of Northwestern tomb construction is that the doorway and entrances to the rear or side chambers of the tomb were made from stone while the walls and ceilings were made of brick. This method of tomb construction was an economical way of providing the same basic template as tombs made completely from stone. This naturally means that all reliefs recovered in the region either decorated the doorway of or entranceways between tomb chambers and helps in estimating the relative position of many scattered and incomplete stones that have been found throughout the region. This mode of construction also allowed for a high degree of standardization in tomb decoration and artisans developed a set repertoire of themes that could and did appear in the same location in many different tombs.[15]

## 2.3    CARVING STYLE AND COLOR

This high degree of standardization was further accomplished through the artisans' use of stencils, a technique that was also exclusive to the production of Eastern Han tomb reliefs from the Northwest. In this region, artists first used stencils to trace the outline of figures with red or black lines after which the area around the figure was reduced to create a level plane. The result is that the same figures or their mirror images appear in different tombs throughout the region.[16]

Artists employed a number of carving styles when creating these images, but most were characterized by deep and shallow relief. Deep relief was more popular initially in the Shanbei region and the background of compositions was cut 2 to 3 centimeters below the surface of the

---

[15] Xin Lixiang and Jiang Yingju, 5-6.

[16] Anthony J. Barbieri-Low, *Artisans in Imperial China* (Seattle: University of Washington Press, 2007), 91-92.

stone. Shallow relief became more prevalent after the move west to Lishi in 140 CE and was used in other areas during the late Eastern Han dynasty, as for example at Yi'nan, Shandong. The Jinxi reliefs, differ from the reliefs at Yi'nan in that the details were not added using incised lines, but created instead using a method peculiar to the Northwest.[17]

After artists had carved out the background of the figures, they added details with red or black ink. Ink was also used in some inscriptions in the region which may account for the small number of tombs that have been discovered with detailed inscriptions. In the final stage, artists could expand their basic palette using black, red, blue, orange/brown and white mineral pigments to add color to the figures. As a result, many of the details of these reliefs are now lost to the firsthand viewer. The traces of this color can still be seen on many of the stones from Dabaodang, Shenmu, Shaanxi.[18]

## 2.4    A BRIEF OVERVIEW OF MAJOR ICONOGRAPHIC FEATURES

Although I offer a detailed analysis of certain aspects of the iconography of stones from the Northwest in what follows, here I will briefly highlight two of their most common characteristics. Although Chinese scholarship has often focused on agricultural scenes and scenes of daily life in these reliefs, the overarching iconography of the Northwest is saturated with imagery relating to the ascension of the soul to paradise. Xiwangmu, Dongwangong and

---

[17] Xin Lixiang and Jiang Yingju, 13-14. Li Jian has also divided reliefs from this region into three types based on their style of carving, composition and motifs. Li Jian, 41-55. Li's analysis, however is hindered by an attempt to fit carving styles into a temporal schema that based on the small number of dated reliefs is tentative at best.

[18] Anthony J. Barbieri-Low, 88; Xin Lixiang and Jiang Yingju, 13-14. See also the color plates in Shaanxi sheng kaogu yanjiusuo  and Yulin shi wenwu guanli wei.

*xian* (immortals) appear in tombs throughout the region along with a number of detailed compositions depicting the journey of the deceased to the Western Paradise[19]. Stone carvers in the both Shaaxni and Shanxi also used ornate vine-like patterns that typically from the border of the relief, but in a few tombs decorate the background of the composition. These designs may have been meant to represent the atmosphere of the immortal world and could have been derived from floral motifs from Central Asia.[20]

## 2.5    A BRIEF HISTORY OF SHANG AND XIHE COMMANDERIES

During the Eastern Han dynasty, most of the major areas of tomb production in Shaanxi and Shanxi were under the administration of Shang and Xihe commanderies. Comprised of isolated, but fertile valleys surrounded by steep mountains and hills, this region was the focus of Qin and Han colonization. During the Qin and Han dynasties, Shang and Xihe commanderies served as an important buffer zone between the Xiongnu Empire and the Qin and Western Han capitals. Through extensive government-sponsored development, they also became major agricultural centers and important traffic hubs between the Han capitals and regions to the north.[21]

---

[19] See for example the lintel over the entrance to the rear room of the tomb of Tian Fang, Sishipu, Suide, Shaanxi. 92 CE. Li Guilong and Wang Jianqin, Fig. 4.

[20] Xin Lixiang and Jiang Yingju, 4-5; Shih Hsio-yen, "Han Stone Tomb Reliefs from Shensi Province," 60-62.

[21] Xin Lixiang and Jiang Yingju, 1-2. See Klass Ruitenbeek, "The Northwestern Style of Eastern Han Pictorial Stone Engravings: The Tomb of Zuo Biao and Other Eastern Han Tombs Near Lishi, Shanxi Province," 133, for a map of these commanderies.

A Shang commandery is first mentioned in the "Qin benji (Basic Annals of Qin)" in the *Shi ji* (*Records of the Grand Historian*) in 361 BCE as a region governed by the state of Wei; parts of this commandery were later annexed by the state of Qin. After unification, Shang commandery became a pivotal region within the Qin Empire when General Meng Tian (d. 210 BCE) was dispatched by the First Emperor to the region. After he took control of the lands south of the Yellow River and pushed the nomadic forces back across the Yin Mountains, Meng Tian lived in Shang commandery for ten years and built border defenses and forty-four walled district cities.[22]

During the Qin and Han dynasties, Shang commandery included most of northern Shaanxi extending to the north as far as Wushenqi, Inner Mongolia. The actual control of this area was dependent on the strength of the Han government and during the Eastern Han dynasty northern portions of the province fell under the jurisdiction of Xihe commadery. After the establishment of the Han commanderies of Wuyuan and Shoufang in 127 BCE, Shang commandery supplied the main route of access to the north via the Han Northern Road along the Wuding River past Fushi then north through the Great Wall at Yulin. The seat of government of Shang commandery is a point of contention among scholars who argue that it was either located at Suide or at Fushi, whose location was somewhere to the south of the modern city of Yulin. Both claims are supported by textual records. Regardless of the exact location of the capital,

---

[22] *Shi ji* 5, "Qin benji (Basic Annals of Qin);" *Shi ji* 88, "Meng Tian liezhuan (The Biography of Meng Tian);" *Shi ji* 110 "Xiongnu liezhuan (The Account of the Xiongnu)." Sima Qian, *Shi ji* (Beijing: Zhonghua shuju, 1959 [1973 printing]), 202,206, 2566, 2886. Translations see Sima Qian, *Records of the Grand Historian: Qin Dynasty*, translated by Burton Watson (Hong Kong: Research Centre for Translation, Chinese University of Hong Kong; New York: Renditions-Columbia University Press, 1993), 23, 26 and 207-208, and *Records of the Grand Historian: Han Dynasty II*, translated by Burton Watson (Hong Kong: Research Centre for Translation, Chinese University of Hong Kong; New York: Renditions-Columbia University Press, 1993), 133.

from the distribution of tomb reliefs in the region it is clear that during the Eastern Han dynasty the area from Yulin south to Suide and Mizhi was a major population center.[23]

The area that became Xihe commandery was also originally controlled by the state of Wei and annexed to the state of Qin at the same time as Shang commandery during the Warring States Period (475-221 BCE).[24] Xihe commandery was established in 125 BCE by Wudi (140-87 BCE) and lay on the east and west banks of the Yellow River and included the area around Shenmu, Shaanxi. Until 140 CE the capital of the commandery was located north of the Great Wall at Pingding, probably near present-day Ordos City, Dongsheng, Inner Mongolia. After a major Xiongnu rebellion in 140 CE, it was evacuated and moved east to Lishi.[25]

During the Han dynasty, military and agricultural colonies were established in Xihe commandery and it was a major trading center between the North and the Central Plain.[26] After 50 CE, it gained further importance when the city of Meiji, located near present-day Fugu, Shaanxi, became the compulsory home of the Southern Shanyu (*Nan Shanyu*), the leader of the Southern Xiongnu tribes. Originally the headquarters of the Chief Commandant (*duwei*), during the Western Han dynasty the city became the home of Han officials who were appointed to

---

[23] Rafe DeCrespigny, *Northern Frontier: The Policies and Strategy of the Later Han Empire* (Canberra: Faculty of Asian Studies, Australian National University, 1984), 24-25; Pu Hui, "Qin Han Shang jun zhisuo xiaokao (An Examination of the Seat of Government of Shang Commandery during the Qin and Han Dyansties)," *Tangdu xuekan*, Vol. 24, No. 1 (January 2008), 1-3; Xia Zhengnong, *Ci Hai, suoyin ben* (Shanghai: Shanghai cishu chubanshe,1989), 192; cited in Pu Hui.

[24] *Shi ji* 110, "Xiongnu liezhuan." Sima Qian, *Shi ji*, 2885. Translation see Sima Qian, *Records of the Grand Historian: Han Dynasty II*, 133; Watson mistranscribes Xihe as Hexi (Gansu), but it is clearly Xihe in the received texts.

[25] Rafe DeCrespigny, 25; Lu Guilan, "Qin Han shiqi dui Shanbei fazhan (The Development of Shanbei during the Qin and Han Periods)," *Wenbo* 1984(3), 25.

[26] Wang Zijin, "Xihe jun jianzhi yu Handai shan sha jiaotang (The Establishment of Xihe Commmandery and Mountain-Desert Traffic During the Han Dynasty)," *Jinyang xuekan* 1990(6), 78-83.

supervise the government of the Shanyu. The official primarily responsible for this task was given the title of the General of the Gentlemen of the Household Emissary to the Xiongnu (*Shi Xiongnu zhongliang jiang*). [27] The first reliefs found in Shanxi in 1919 are from the tomb of a clerk who served under this official. [28] Rafe DeCrespigny describes the relative position of Han officials and the Southern Shanyu after 50 CE,

> Like a British Resident in a princely state in the time of the Indian empire, Duan Chen (the first official appointed as General of the Gentlemen of the Household Emissary to the Xiongnu) and his successors had ultimate authority over the government of the Southern Xiongnu: they were agents of the Han at this court, they took part in discussion of policy, and they checked his decision and orders to ensure that they were acceptable to the Han. [29]

After 50 CE, the Southern Shanyu became a Han puppet, guided by the emissary and his staff of administrators and secretaries, backed initially by a force of 2500 troops, with an additional 50 troops assigned to serve as "bodyguards" to the Shanyu. [30] This show of force was no doubt designed to ensure the allegiance to the Han of successive Shanyus, whose loyalty continued to waver throughout the first and second centuries CE.

This unstable and unequal relationship continued until 140 when, after a major Xiongnu uprising, an imperial edict ordered the evacuation of the capital of Xihe from Pingding to Lishi. At the same time the administration of Shang commandery was moved south to Xiayang. A similar situation had occurred during the first Qiang Rebellion in 111 CE, but after the rebellion was suppressed the capitals were restored and resettled in the 120s. The abandonment of the capitals of Shang and Xihe commanderies in 140, however, represented the end of Chinese

---

[27] Rafe DeCrespigny, 25, 238.
[28] Klaas Ruitenbeek, "The Northwestern Style of Eastern Han Pictorial Stone Engravings: The Tomb of Zuo Biao and Other Eastern Han Tombs Near Lishi, Shanxi Province," 135.
[29] Rafe DeCrespigny, 238-239.
[30] Ibid., 239.

control of most of the Northern Frontier. [31] It also signaled the end of the contruction of decorated tombs in the Shanbei area, with potential consumers of such tombs fleeing to the south or east. The last datable tomb inscription in the region reads 139.

After 140, the Xiongnu and other nomadic peoples re-occupied the area north of the loop of the Yellow River, driving the Chinese back into the Wei River Valley and the southwestern portions of Xihe commandery. Some attempts at reconstruction by ambitious officials occurred after the late 140s, but their efforst were short-lived. Although the Southern Shanyu was re-established as a Han vassal, his influence was probably nominal because it was no longer clear how many of the nomadic groups in the region still swore allegiance to him. [32] Based on historical records and the continued construction of decorated tombs, the southwestern portion of Xihe around the capital of Lishi remained a viable Han military and cultural center until the end of the 170s. By the late 180s, Han control of the region collapsed and these tombs, their patrons and the unique culture of the Han Northern Frontier were confined to the annals of history.

## 2.6    LIFE IN SHANG AND XIHE COMMANDERIES I: COLONIZATION, DEVELOPMENT AND DECLINE

At the beginning of the Qin dynasty, the areas governed by Shang and Xihe commmanderies were underpopulated and underdeveloped. The defense of the region and the large number of Qin and Han soldiers stationed in these commanderies necessitated the development of their infrastructure, agriculture and economy. Beginning in the Qin dynasty,

---

[31] Ibid., 103, 311.
[32] Ibid., 122, 311-312, 315.

large numbers of people were moved to the north from the interior, foreshadowing policies later implemented during the Han.[33] During the Han dynasty the government encouraged agricultural development on the frontier through the establishment of *tun tian*, military colonies where soldiers farmed during the agricultural season and defended the border during the rest of the year. To increase the number of soldiers manning the frontier garrisons, the government reduced the sentences of criminals who became soldiers along the frontier.[34]

Ultimately the government hoped that these garrisons, combined with a massive influx of civilians, would stabilize Shang and Xihe commanderies and make them self-sufficient. One of the largest government-sponsored emigration of civilians from the interior to the Northern Frontier occurred in 120 BCE:

> 其明年，山東被水菑，民多饑乏，於是天子遣使者虛郡國倉廥以振貧民。猶不足，又募豪富人相貸假。尚不能相救，乃徙貧民於關以西，及充朔方以南新秦中，七十餘萬口，衣食皆仰給縣官。數歲，假予產業，使者分部護之，冠蓋相望。其費以億計，不可勝數.

> The next year (120 BC) the lands east of the mountains were troubled by floods and many of the people were reduced to starvation. The emperor dispatched envoys to the provinces and kingdoms to empty the granaries and relieve the sufferings of the poor, but there was not enough food to go around. He then called upon wealthy families to make loans to the needy, but even this did not remedy the situation. At last he ordered some 700,000 of the poor to emigrate and resettle the lands west of the Pass and the region of New Qin south of Shuofang. Food and clothing were supplied to them for the first few years by the government officials, who were also instructed to lend them what they needed to start a livelihood. Envoys sent to supervise the various groups of emigrants poured out of the capital in such numbers that their cart and carriage covers were constantly in sight of each other on the roads. The expenses of the move were estimated in the billions, the final sum reaching incalculable proportions.[35]

---

[33] See Lu Guilan for an overview of Qin policy, 25-26.

[34] Xin Lixiang and Jiang Yingju, 3.

[35] The region known as New Qin during the Han dynasty included Shang and Xihe commanderies. *Shi ji* 30, "Pingzhun shu (The Treatise on the Balanced Standard)." Sima Qian, *Shi ji*, 1425. Translation see Sima Qian, *Records of the Grand Historian: Han Dynasty II*, 68.

As this passage and the Han policy of reducing criminal sentences for military service suggests,

forced migration to the North also helped to the rid the interior of unwanted social elements. In

114 BCE, in order to further encourage immigration, residents were also allowed to raise horses

and were exempted from the reports on levies and wealth.[36]

The success of such policies during the Western Han is reflected in the census of 2 CE

that records the population of Shang commandery at 606,658 and that of Xihe at 698,836. Many

of these residents probably included peasant farmers who had moved to the area to take

advantage of its fertile farmland made possible through extensive Han irrigation projects or to

breed and herd animals. Others may have moved there to work in the salt fields in Qiuci, north of

Yulin.[37] The benefits to those living in the region were nostalgically described by Yu Xu in a

memorial to Shundi in 129 CE:

> 且沃野千里，穀稼殷積，又有龜茲鹽池以為民利。水草豐美，土宜產牧，牛
> 馬銜尾，群羊塞道...
>
> Fertile ground stretches for a thousand *li* with abundant and flourishing crops of
> grain, and there are also the salt ponds of Qiuci which provide a source of profit
> to the people. With abundant water and splendid pasturage, suitable for the
> breeding of animals, with herds of cattle and horses head to tail, and flocks of
> sheep so many that they block the roads...[38]

Land of plenty or not, the region was neglected and pilfered during the Wang Mang Interregnum

(8-23 CE). A passage in the "Wang Mang liezhuan (Biography of Wang Mang)" in the *Han shu*

---

[36] *Shi ji* 30, "Pingzhun shu." Sima Qian, *Shi ji*, 1438. Translation see Sima Qian, *Records of the Grand Historian: Han Dynasty II*, 79.

[37] These population figures are recorded in *Han Shu* 28, "Dili zhi xia (Treatise on Geogrpahy, Part 2)." Ban Gu, *Han shu* (Beijing: Zhonghua shuju, 1968), 1617-1618; Rafe DeCrespigny, 244; Lu Guilan, 26.

[38] *Hou Han Shu* 87/77, "Xi Qiang zhuan (Account of the Western Qiang)." Fan Ye, *Hou Han shu* (*History of the Former Han Dynasty*) (Beijing: Zhonghua shu ju: Xin hua shu dian, 1965 [1973 printing]), 2893. Translation by Rafe DeCrespigny, 116.

(*History of the Former Han Dynasty*) describes the circumstances that faced many commoners living in the region in 11 CE:

> 是時諸將在邊，須大眾集，吏士放縱，而內郡愁於徵發，民棄城郭流亡為盜賊，并州、平州尤甚.

> At that time (11 CE), while the various generals who were at the border were waiting for large bands [of soldiers] to be collected, their officers and soldiers did as they pleased, while the inner commanderies were troubled with levying [troops] and collecting [materials]. The common people left the cities and suburbs and became vagrants, becoming thieves and robbers. They were especially numerous in the provinces of Bing [the location of Shang and Xihe commanderies] and Ping.[39]

During Wang Mang's reign, inconsistent and unrealistic policies together with extensive corruption led to the migration of settlers to the south allowing the Xiongnu and other foreign tribes to reclaim the Northern Frontier. The civil wars that followed and the reestablishment of the Han dynasty in 25 CE did little to stabilize the region which remained under the control of Xiongnu tribes, bandits and warlords.

It was not until 50 CE, with the surrender of the Southern Shanyu and his forced migration south to Meiji, that an imperial edict ordered the resettlement of the North. Officials, together with convicts with reduced sentences, were sent to repair and occupy the old defenses. The government issued grants of money and grain to encourage refugees from the North to return to their former homes. Although some returned, it does not appear that the government possessed the administrative resources to force the massive relocation of settlers to the region. Seven years later, Mingdi (28-75) issued an official edict abandoning the project.[40]

---

[39] *Han Shu* 99, "Wang Mang liezhuan zhong (The Biography of Wang Mang, Part 2)." Ban Gu, *Han Shu*, 4125. Translation based on Ban Gu, *The History of the Former Han Dynasty*, translated by Homer H. Dubs (Baltimore: Waverly Press, 1955), 3: 313-314.
[40] Rafe DeCrespigny, 242-243.

Based on historical sources, the extent to which Shang and Xihe commanderies were ever fully resettled during the first and second centuries is difficult to determine. The last major push to resettle and develop the Northern Frontier occurred around 130; but the government's efforts at this time focused on repairs to existing fortifications and the irrigation of land to insure the self-sufficiency of *tun tian*.[41] These initiatives suggest that, by the year 130, the existence of a civilian population or the reconstitution of one in the North was no longer a priority of the Han government.

Population figures recorded in the *Hou Han Shu* (*History of the Later Han Dynasty*) for the year 140 also suggest that either the Northern Frontier had never substantially regained its population or that those who had immigrated had once again fled to the south. Compared to the figures recorded in the *Han Shu* in 2 CE (Shang commandery: 606,658; Xihe: 698,836), the "Junguo zhi (Treatise on Administrative Geography) " in the *Hou Han Shu* records a sharp decline in the population of both commanderies with Shang commandery registering at 28,599 and Xihe at 20,838. Such low numbers are the result of the Xiongnu uprising that occurred in the same year as the census, changes to the county structure within the commanderies and include only those who were living in the region who could be registered. Figures for other frontier commanderies also demonstrate a similar decline in population, implying an overall failure of the Eastern Han government to re-establish civilian colonies on its northern and western frontiers.[42]

These low population figures can certainly be seen as a sign of the precarious condition of life on the Northern Frontier. In Shang and Xihe commanderies for more than a century farming and the local economy were repeatedly interrupted by rebellions and raids and the

---

[41] *Hou Han Shu* 87/77, "Xi Qiang zhuan (The Account of the Western Qiang)." Fan Ye, 2893.
[42] Rafe DeCrespigny, 242-245; *Hou Han shu* 113/23, "Junguo zhi (Treatise on Administrative Geography)." Fan Ye, 3524.

sometimes more disastrous ensuing imperial campaigns. This situation, according to Wang Fu

(d. 163 CE), an official born in Anding commandery (modern Gansu), was exacerbated by the

corruption, brutality and ineptitude of local officials who caused famine and death by

misappropriating grain and other supplies while misleading the court with false reports of

success.[43]

Although the *Hou Han shu* offers a bleak picture of life on the Northern Frontier during

the Eastern Han dynasty, tomb reliefs and inscriptions provide an alternate source of information

regarding life in Shang and Xihe commanderies. Rather than presenting scenes of desolation and

woe, these reliefs suggest a thriving (although perhaps idealized) local economy based on

agriculture, hunting, animal breeding and herding. These tombs also provide evidence for the

strength of an economy that supported specialized artisans, and perhaps even a number of

competing workshops.[44] At the same time, the number of tombs and scattered reliefs found in

this region suggests a substantial consumer base whose constituents had the means and leisure to

prepare for the afterlife.[45] This suggests that Han attempts at resettlement were not completely

unsuccessful and during parts of the first and second centuries CE, the general political, cultural

and economic climate of Shang and Xihe commanderies was not as depressing as accounts in the

*Hou Han shu* suggest.

---

[43] Rafe DeCrespigny, 114.

[44] Several different contemporary carving styles suggest that there may have been competing
workshops in this region. Compare for example the figures in the reliefs from the tomb of the
Liaodong *taishou* (Grand Administrator of Liaodong) (d. 90) to those in the tomb of Tian Fang
(d. 92). See Li Guilong and Wang Jianqin, *Suide Handai huaxiang shi* (*Han Dynasty Tomb
Reliefs from Shaanxi*) (Xi'an: Shaanxi renmin meishu chubanshe, 2001), 14-21 and 36-42.

[45] The inscription from the tomb of Zuo Biao makes it clear that he planned the tomb before his
death, as do several other inscriptions from tombs in the Shanbei area. Ruitenbeek, 135.

The polarized accounts of life along the Northern Frontier that we find in the archaeological and historical sources are the result of two major factors. Information provided in the *Hou Han Shu* frequently occurs in episodes related to rebellions and warfare. These passages show a clear Confucian bias that views the existence of Han colonies in the North and the West at best as a misuse of state funds, and places life in the North in the worst possible light. The tomb reliefs, in constrast, provide an idealized version of life along the Northern Frontier and many, as I will argue below, were probably constructed during the height of Han settlement in the region. As such, they provide glimpses of life along the frontier during what probably were literally the best of times when the region was stable enough to support large communities of Han Chinese. It may also be that the wealth of the region was concentrated among the consumers of these tombs who reaped the rewards of Han colonization, the benefits of which were less apparent to the average inhabitants of these commanderies.

Inscriptions from these tombs provide clues to the height of Han settlement in the Shanbei area (Table 1). Of the total number of inscriptions found in the region, ten fall between the years 90 and 107. Although this may result from random finds, similarities in carving style and motif imply that many reliefs excavated in the Shanbei region were made within this time period. This suggests that the initial Han re-settlement policies instituted in the 50s were fairly successful and by the 90s the region was supporting a number of thriving Chinese communities.

Shortly after the year 107 it appears this period of general stability and tomb building came to an end. Although two inscriptions have been found with later dates (128, 139) in the Shanbei area, the sudden decline in datable tomb inscriptions after 107 suggests major political, social and economic upheaval on the Northern Frontier. The beginning of this period corresponds roughly to first Qiang Rebellion (107-118). This revolt spread across parts of Liang and Bing Provinces where both Shang and Xihe commanderies were located. The rebellion and the subsequent policies of the Eastern Han government had a horrible impact on the people living in these provinces.[46] The *Hou Han shu* records that,

百姓戀土，不樂去舊，遂乃刈其禾稼，發徹室屋，夷營壁，破積聚…

> The common people were attached to their land and reluctant to leave their homes, So [troops were sent in to] break down their crops, demolish their houses, raze their walls and palisades, and destroy their supplies and stores...[47]

Although this account is influenced by the anti-government sentiments of Wang Fu's *Qianfu lun* (*Comments of a Recluse*), it is easy to imagine the difficulty of both rich and poor settlers living in a region that was repeatedly threatened by nomadic incursions and short-sighted government policies. This instability eventually made it easier for many to relocate to greener pastures, but the *Hou Han shu* and later tomb inscriptions confirm that some individuals did stay or returned to the region in the 120s. Eventually, they were faced with another major Xiongnu rebellion in 140 and the evacuation of the capitals of the commanderies to the south and east. From the reliefs and inscriptions found in the east in Shanxi we know that a number of officials and some artisans made this move. Until more tombs in the region are discovered, however, it is reasonable to conclude that that the Eastern Han colonies in modern Shanxi were not as extensive as their earlier counterparts and were comprised primarily of Han civil and military officials and northern nomadic peoples. These two groups, even at the height of Han settlement, formed the core population of Shang and Xihe commanderies and it is to them that we will now turn.

---

[46] Rafe DeCrespigny, 103-104, 144.

[47] *Hou Han Shu* 87/77, "Xi Qiang zhuan (The Account of the Western Qiang)." Fan Ye, 2888. Translation see Rafe DeCrespigny, 103-104.

## 2.7    LIFE IN SHANG AND XIHE COMMANDERIES II: OFFICIALS, SOLDIERS AND BARBARIANS

Although during the Han dynasty Shang and Xihe commanderies were home to a variety of Han Chinese from various backgrounds, the very reason for their prescene in the region meant that this population had a strong military as well as foreign component. In the final section of this chapter I will highlight the general characteristics of the Eastern Han military apparatus along the Northern Frontier and the centrality of warfare to life in Shang and Xihe commanderies. I will conclude by surveying the non-Han Chinese population living in the region.

Despite the military reforms instituted at the beginning of the Eastern Han dynasty, the nature and composition of the armies along the Northern Frontier does not appear to have been significantly different from their Western Han counterparts. In this region, residents continued to be called for compulsory military training, and service and troops were recruited from the interior to fill posts in the garrisons and standing armies posted along the frontier. These standing armies were organized into three camps: 1) the Camp of the General Who Crosses the Liao (*Du Liao jiangjun*), 2) the Camp of the Colonel Who Protects the Wuhuan (*Hu Wuhuan xiaowei*) and 3) the Camp of the Colonel Who Protects the Qiang (*Hu Qiang xiaowei*). Troops stationed along the frontier for a long period of time were voluntarily transferred at the end of a period of conscription or recruited from the permanent Eastern Han military camp at Liyang which served as a professional reserve and became a major source of troops for the General Who Crosses the Liao. Garrisons that defended the Northern Frontier continued to be made up of recruits stationed there for long periods of time-- either criminals or conscripts pardoned from death sentences, professional soldiers (volunteers paid salaries by the state) and non-Han Chinese troops. In times of emergency, these forces were supplemented by commandery troops raised from the general population.[48]

Although troop numbers would have varied based on circumstances, it is clear that the military formed a key component of the population of Shang and Xihe commanderies. The centrality of the military establishment in the region is confirmed by three Eastern Han tomb inscriptions that identify the deceased as connected to the military: 1) Niu Liping (d.139) who held the military position of *wei* (commandant), 2) Wang Junwei who was a *shizhe* (scribe) under the Colonel Who Protects the Wuhuan and 3) Zuo Biao (d.150) who served as a scribe at the military headquarters of the General of the Gentleman of the Household Emissary to the Xiongnu.[49]

Other inscriptions from the region record the deceased as holding positions under the *taishou* (grand administrator) of Xihe. Although technically part of the civilian administration, passages from the *Hou Han shu* suggest that the taishou of Xihe had a number of military responsibilities as well.[50] Considering the numer of soldiers and military officials in the region,

---

[48] Rafe DeCrespigny, 50, 253-254; Mark Edward Lewis, "The Han Abolition of Universal Military Service," In *Warfare in Chinese History*, edited by Hans van de Ven (Leiden, Boston and Köln: Brill, 2000), 52, 57.  For the practice of employing foreign soldiers in Han armies and/or the Han policy of "Using Foreigners to Control Foreigners (*Yi Yi zhi Yi*)" see Hong Tingyan, "Liang Han Sanguo de 'Yi Bing' (Foreign Soldiers of the Han Dynasty and Three Kingdoms Period)," *Wenshizhe* 1958(3), 29-35; Shangguan xuzhi, "Liang Han zhengzhi 'yi yi zhi yi' cele yunyong de zhuyao fangshi he tedian (The Main Ways and Characteristics of 'Controlling Foreigners by Foreigners' in the Hans)," *Nandu xuetan* 2006(6), 1-6 and Xing Yitian, "Dong Han de hu bing (Eastern Han Barbarian Soldiers)," *Zhengzhi daxue xuebao* 1973(12), 143-166.

[49] Klass Ruitenbeek, "The Northwestern Style of Eastern Han Pictorial Stone Engravings: The Tomb of Zuo Biao and Other Eastern Han Tombs Near Lishi, Shanxi Province," 135-136.

[50] *Hou Han Shu*, Chapters 16/6, "Deng Kou liezhuan (The Biography of Deng Yu, Deng Xun, Kou Xun and Kou Rong);" 22/12 "Zhu You, Jing Dan, Wang Liang, Du Mao, Ma Cheng, Liu Long, Fu Jun, Jian Tan,  Ma Wu liezhuan (The Biography of Zhu You, Jing Dan, Wang Liang,

the many unknown individuals buried in tombs in the Northwest would possibley have also have

dealt with the military establishment on a regular basis. They may have also been called in turn

to serve in the local militia. Unlike residents of the inner commanderies, where compulsory

military training and service had been abolished, residents along the Northern Frontier continued

to follow a system of compulsory service and militia training. Unlike during the Western Han

dynasty, however, they did not serve annual terms in the garrisons, but were called in to deal

with small-scale banditry, raiding and to supplement elite troops during invasions.[51]

The centrality of the military to the culture of Shang and Xihe commanderies is remarked

upon by the *Han Shu*:

> 及安定、北地、上郡、西河，皆迫近戎狄，修習戰備，高上氣力…漢興，六
> 郡良家子選給羽林、期門，以材力為官，名將多出焉.

> As for Anding, Beidi, Xihe and Shang commanderies, all are compelled by the
> closeness of the Rong and Di to practice combat readiness. They esteem moral
> integrity and physical strength. They consider hunting and using the bow and
> arrow as the highest (skill)… After the re-establishment of the Han dynasty, sons
> from the best families from these commanderies were selected to fill the offices of
> the Feathered Forest and the Qimen with capable officials; a number of famous
> generals were born there…[52]

Based on the popularity of the figure of the mounted archer in tombs from the Northwest, we

know that this unique culture continued to thrive during the Eastern Han dynasty.

---

Du Mao, Ma Cheng, Liu Long, Fu Jun  Jian Tan and Ma Wu);" 89/79, "Nan Xiongnu liezhuan
(Account of the Southern Xiongnu)." Fan Ye, 602, 779, 2952-2953, 2955.

[51] Based on historical records, it may be more accurate to say that the Western Han system was
modified rather than truly abolished. During the Eastern Han dynasty, even in the interior,
commandery troops were still called in times of emergency, however their knowledge of warfare
(due to the abolition of military training and reviews) was considerably less than conscripted
troops during the Western Han. Commandery troops in the North were similarly only called on
in times of crises. Owing to the precarious nature of life along the Northern Frontier, this must
have happened far more frequently than in the interior. Rafe DeCrespigny, 50; Mark Edward
Lewis, "The Han Abolition of Universal Military Service," 52, 54.

[52] *Han Shu* 28, "Dili zhi xia (The Treatise on Geography, Part 2)." Ban Gu, *Han Shu*, 1644.

As the *Han Shu* implies, this regional culture was necessitated and intensified by, "the closeness of the Rong and Di." To the patrons of these images, however, these "barbarians" were not a threat that remained behind the Great Wall occasionally invading and pillaging, they were also neighbors. From the beginning of the Han dynasty, the Northern Frontier was populated by many "loyal barbarians" who were an essential part of the maintenance and protection of Shang and Xihe commanderies and whose numbers and constituents fluctuated during the Western and Eastern Han.[53] Although greater numbers of tribes began immigrating to the area with the decline of the Han-Chinese population in the mid-second century, many were originally forced to immigrate into the region after they surrendered to the Han government and were placed under the jurisdiction of a *shuguo* (Dependent State) administered by a *duwei* (Chief Commandant). Five Dependent States were first created in 121 BCE after a large number of Xiongnu surrendered to Huo Qubing (140-117 BCE) and were resettled across the Northern Frontier. Sometime after this, a dependent state was established in Shang commandery with its administrative seat at Qiuci (previously mentioned as the location of numerous salt ponds). As the name itself implies, this state was probably inhabited by people from the Central Asian kingdom of Kucha (Qiuci guo in Chinese) who had surrendered to the Han government. The *Hou Han Shu* confirms the existence of a Dependent State of Qiuci during the Eastern Han dynasty, listing it as a subdivision of Shang commandery. In 55 BCE, Dependent States were again established to incorporate surrendered Xiongnu.[54]

---

[53] See *Shi ji* 110, "Xiongnu liezhuan," for the loyal barbarians of Shang commandery who were appointed in the early part of the second century BCE to defend the frontier. Sima Qian, *Shi ji*, 2895. Translation see Sima Qian, *Records of the Grand Historian: Han Dynasty II*, 140.
[54] Peter Boodberg, "Two Notes on the History of the Chinese Frontier," *Harvard Journal of Asiatic Studies*, Vol. 1, No. 3/4 (November 1936), 286-287; Pu Hui, "Liang Han Shangjun Qiuci

Although the offices of the military commanders of the Western Han Dependent States were abolished by Aidi (7-1 BCE) at the end of the first century BCE, the Dependent States of Shang and Xihe commanderies were officially re-established in 90 CE. These administrative units were probably intended to control the Xiongnu groups that had surrendered alongside the Southern Shanyu and the other non-Han groups living in the region. An Eastern Han innovation to the policy of creating Dependent States was the creation of the three camps along the frontier mentioned above that were established along with the internal resettlement of several tribes.[55] Many passages in the *Hou Han Shu* refer to groups of Xiongnu, Qiang and Wusun from Shang and Xihe commanderies. Although it is impossible to establish an accurate timeline regarding the decline of the Han population along the Northern Frontier, it is safe to suggest that when many of these reliefs were produced the Han Chinese living in Shang and Xihe commanderies were outnumbered by non-Chinese tribesman.

## 2.8    CONCLUSION

This chapter has provided an overview of the historical context in which Eastern Han tombs were produced in Shaanxi and Shanxi. The most extensive survey of its kind, it has attempted to use tomb inscriptions and reliefs to fill some of the gaps in the historical record and to give a more nuanced account of life along the Northern Frontier. I have shown that these tombs were created in a region inhabited by mainly non-Han Chinese and colonized by the Qin

---

shuguo ji qi wenhua yi cun kao yi (An Examination of the Han Dependent State of Qiuci and Its Culture)," *Renwen zazhi* 2008(5), 130-138.
[55] Mark Edward Lewis, "The Han Abolition of Universal Military Service," 57-59.

and Han governments. This unique atmosphere created a regional culture that emphasized martial prowess. Based on the above passage in the *Han shu* and the predominance of hunting scenes in tomb reliefs from the Northwest, we can suppose that martial valor in the region was epitomized by the figure of the mounted archer.  In what follows I will argue that 1) the figure of the mounted archer was a significant marker of status and belonging among Han Chinese living along the Northern Frontier and 2) in tombs from the Northwest this figure became an active component of images ensuring the safe passage of the deceased to paradise.

# TABLE 1. INSCRIPTIONS FOUND IN TOMBS FROM SHAANXI AND SHANXI

| Name | Official Title | Date | Tomb Site |
|---|---|---|---|
| Unknown[56] | 遼東太守 (Grand Administrator of Liaodong) | 90 | Huangjiata 黃家塔 Tomb No. 7, Suide, Shaanxi |
| Tian Fang 田鈁 [57] | 西河太守都集掾 (Division Head 掾史 of Collection都集 Under the Grand Administrator of Xihe)[58] | 92 | Sishipu 四十鋪, Suide, Shaanxi |
| Yang Mengyuan杨孟元 [59] | 西河太守行長史事离石守長 (District Chief 守長 of Lishi Responsible to the Chief Clerk 長史 and Usher 行 of the Grand Administrator of Xihe) | 6 | Sujiagetuo 蘇家圪坨, Suide, Shaanxi |
| Xu Wuling 徐無令 [60] | | 98 | Sishipu 四十鋪, Suide, Shaanxi |
| Wang Deyuan 王得元 [61] | | 100 | Xiancheng ximenwai 縣城西門外, Suide, Shaanxi |
| Guo Zhiwen 郭稚文 [62] | | 103 | Wulidian 五裡店, Suide, Shaanxi |
| Ren Xiaosun 任孝孙 [63] | 西河太守掾 (Division Head/Official under the Grand Administrator of Xihe) | 104 | Sishipu 四十鋪, Suide, Shaanxi |
| Zhang Wenqing張文卿 [64] | | 104 | Baijiashan 百家山, Suide, Shaanxi |

---

[56] Li Guilong and Wang Jianqin, 6.

[57] Ibid., 6.

[58] Kang Lanying and Wang Zhian, "Shaanxi Suide xian sishilipu huaxiang shi mu diaocha jianbao (A Brief Report on the Tomb Excavated at Sishilipu, Suide, Shaanxi)," *Kaogu yu wenwu* 2002(3), 23.

[59] Li Guilong and Wang Jianqin, 6.

[60] Ibid.

[61] Ibid.

[62] Ibid.

[63] Ibid.

[64] Ibid.

| Name | Title | Plate | Location |
| --- | --- | --- | --- |
| Wang Shengxu 王聖序 [65] | | 104 | Huangjiata Tomb No. 6, Suide, Shaanxi |
| Tian Wencheng 田文成 [66] | 西河太守掾 (Division Head/Official under the Grand Administrator of Xihe) | 106 | Sishipu, Suide, Shaanxi |
| Niu Wenming 牛文明 [67] | | 107 | Guanzhuang 官莊 Tomb No. 4, Mizhi, Shaanxi |
| Unknown[68] | | 128 | Liujiawan 刘家湾, Suide, Shaanxi |
| Sima Shu 司馬叔?[69] | | 138 | Hejiagou 賀家溝, Qingjian, Shaanxi |
| Niu Liping 牛李平 [70] | 西河内山陽尉 (Commandant of Shanyang, Xihe) | 139 | Shangzhuang 尚莊, Mizhi, Shaanxi |
| Unknown[71] | | | Huangjiata Tomb No. 8, Suide, Shaanxi |
| Guo Zhongli 郭仲理 [72] | | | Shanbei, Unknown |
| Guo Lifei 郭李妃 [73] | | | Shanbei, Unknown or near Lishi, Shanxi? |
| Niu Jun 牛君 [74] | | | Mizhi, Shaanxi |

---

[65] Ibid.

[66] Ibid.

[67] Li Lin, Kang Lanying and Zhao Liguang, 24. No official title mentioned.

[68] Li Guilong and Wang Jianqin, 6.

[69] Li Lin, Kang Lanying and Zhao Liguang, 220. 4 characters indecipherable. 司馬 could be the person family name or the title of a military official. 叔 seem to have probably been part of some proper noun.

[70] Ibid., 53, 234

[71] Ibid., 123.

[72] Ibid., 234.

[73] Ibid., 202; says stone was found in Shanbei area around 1920; however Wang Jinyuan, "Lishi Han huaxiang shi (Han Dynasty Tomb Reliefs from Lishi)," *Wenwu shijie* 2002(1), 60 says it was found near Lishi.

| Name | Title | Date | Location |
| --- | --- | --- | --- |
| Unknown [75] | | | Sishipu, Suide |
| Gu Xiaoqing 賈孝卿 [76] | 西河太守鹽官掾 (Official in the Office of Salt of the Grand Administrator of Xihe) | | Hejiagou, Qingjian, Shaanxi |
| Unknown [77] | | | Huangjiata Tomb No. 1, Suide, Shaanxi |
| Wang Junwei 王君威? [78] | 使者持节護烏桓校尉 (Scribe in the Memorial Section of the Colonel Who Protects the Wuhuan) | | HuangjiaTomb No. 4, Suide, Shaanxi |
| Unknown [79] | | | Wuyanquan 嗚嚥泉, Suide, Shaanxi |
| Wu Zhizhong 吴执仲 [80] | 漢☒ 東掾丞 (Assistant to the Division Head of Hedong?) | | Jiaokouzhen 交口鎮, Lishi, Shanxi |
| Unknown [81] | | | Shipan 石盤 Tomb No. 16, Shanxi |
| Unknown [82] | | | Shipan Tomb No. 8, Shanxi |
| Zuo Biao 左表 [83] | 使者持節中郎将莫府奏曹史 (Scribe in the Memorials Section at the Military Headquarters of the Leader and Court Gentleman and Envoy Holding the Tasseled Staff) | 150 | Near Lishi, Shanxi |
| Sun Daren 孙大 | 漢故花陽令 (Prefect of Huayang) | 171 | Mamaozhuang 馬茂莊, Shanxi |

---


[74] Li Lin, Kang Lanying and Zhao Liguang, 36.

[75] Ibid., 100

[76] Ibid., 234.

[77] Ibid.

[78] Li Guilong and Wang Jianqin, 127

[79] Li Lin, Kang Lanying and Zhao Liguang, 135.

[80] Dong Louping and Yang Shaoshun, "Shanxi Luliang diqu zhengji de Han huaxiang shi (Han Dynasty Tomb Reliefs from the Luliang area in Shanxi)," *Wenwu* 2008(7), 84.

[81] Wang Jinyuan, "Shanxi Lishi Shipan Handai huaxiang shi mu (Tombs with Han Dynasty Tomb Reliefs from Shipan, Lishi, Shanxi)," *Wenwu* 2005(2), 44, 50.

[82] Ibid.

[83] Klass Ruitenbeek, "The Northwestern Style of Eastern Han Pictorial Stone Engravings: The Tomb of Zuo Biao and Other Eastern Han Tombs Near Lishi, Shanxi Province," 135.

| 人 [84] | | | |
|---|---|---|---|
| Niu Chan 牛產 [85] | 西河圜陽守令 (District Magistrate of Huanyang, Xihe) | 175 | Mamaozhuang Tomb No. 14, Shanxi |
| Unknown [86] | 西河太守... ([Of the] Grand Administrator of Xihe) | | Shipan Tomb No. 18, Shanxi |

[84] Wang Jinyuan, "Lishi Han huaxiang shi," 60.

[85] Klass Ruitenbeek, "The Northwestern Style of Eastern Han Pictorial Stone Engravings: The Tomb of Zuo Biao and Other Eastern Han Tombs Near Lishi, Shanxi Province," 135.

[86] Ibid., 135-136.

**3.0 HUNTING IMAGERY IN EASTERN HAN TOMBS: MAJOR CATEGORIES, GEOGRAPHICAL DISTRIBUTION AND PREVIOUS INTERPRETATIONS**

In this chapter I establish the regional characteristics of hunting imagery in Eastern Han tombs and highlight the unique features of scenes of the hunt from Shaanxi and Shanxi. During this period, scenes of the hunt can be divided into four types: 1) hunters on foot accompanied by hounds, 2) archer(s) shooting at birds or monkeys in a tree, 3) human-animal combat and 4) archers or figures carrying other weapons on horseback. On another level, these scenes can be further separated into imagery that depicts quotidian hunting scenes and that which includes fantastic elements such as immortals, mythical beasts and deities. Previous scholarship has often assumed that such imagery is homogenous offering broad interpretations that ignore its diversity. Scholars who have focused on specific types of hunting scenes often essentialize the significance of motifs to different patrons and viewers.

Based on the prevalence of these motifs, four regional clusters show preferences for sets of imagery. These include tomb reliefs and tomb bricks from the modern provinces of 1) Shandong, Jiangsu, and Anhui, 2) Nanyang, Luoyang, Henan, 3) Sichuan, and 4) Shaanxi and Shanxi (the Northwest). I will briefly outline these preferences to establish that in comparison to other regions, scenes of the hunt from the Northwest were dominated by two major characteristics: 1) a strong preference for scenes with mounted archers and 2) a tendency to combine and conflate motifs of immortality with scenes of the hunt. After establishing the geographical spread of these motifs, I will review and critique past interpretations of Eastern Han hunting imagery and more specific explanations of the hunt in reliefs from the Shaanxi and Shanxi. Previous scholarship has failed to take into account the regional characteristics of hunting imagery during this period and has interpreted scenes of the hunt as status markers and reflections of contemporary life. I instead will argue that images of the hunt from the Northwest do not depict the leisure activities of an upper class, but were placed in the tomb to aid the journey of the deceased to paradise.


## 3.1   HUNTING IMAGERY IN SHANDONG, JIANGSU AND ANHUI


Scenes of the hunt in Eastern Han tomb reliefs excavated from the modern provinces of Shandong, Jiangsu and Anhui typically illustrate: 1) hunters on foot accompanied by hounds or 2) archer(s) shooting at birds or monkeys in a tree. These motifs decorate underground reliefs, above-ground shrines and *que* pillars/gates. The most common elements are hunters, with or without hounds, which can be seen in the bottom register of a relief from a shrine at Jiaxiang, Shandong.[87] On the right, two hounds chase two rabbits and are followed by two hunters carrying nets; on the left another man holds a hound on a leash. In other reliefs hunters carry nets, crossbows, bows and/or spears. Some scenes may include hunters on horseback or fishing scenes.[88] The number and kinds of landscape elements included in these reliefs vary from the

---

[87] *Zhonguo huaxiang shi quanji*, Vol. 2, Fig. 125.
[88] *Zhonguo huaxiang shi quanji*, Vol. 1, Figs. 95 and 104.

blank background found in the relief from Jiaxiang to those in which hunters are clearly depicted in the mountains.

Although scenes of the hunt in Shandong, Jiangsu and Anhui are far from homogenous, many depict hunting hounds. Based on funerary goods, historical anecdotes and ritual texts, dogs played three major roles in the life and death of individuals in Han and pre-Han China. These included their use in hunting, their role as guardians and as a source of food for meals or sacrifices.[89] Dogs were prized as hunting companions during the Shang dynasty (c.1500- 1050 BCE) and Western Zhou (1050-770 BCE) ,[90] and to judge from Qin and Han dynasty texts, continued to play a major role in the chase. In hunting scenes from Shandong and other areas, the appearance of these dogs is similar to that of the modern greyhound and they are most often shown hunting rabbits. These dogs can be compared to those represented by ceramic figurines and depicted on pottery towers and tomb reliefs that are larger guard dogs who were the predecessors to the modern Chow and other large regional breeds in present-day China.[91]

The inclusion of hounds as active companions in hunting scenes highlights the quotidian nature of hunting imagery in Shandong, Jiangsu and Anhui. Many scenes also appear to illustrate leisurely hunts in the countryside, devoid of any real dangers. The exception to this general role can be seen in several reliefs from Anqiu, Shandong, in which hunters appear to be battling real

---

[89] Virginia Bower, "Figure of a Dog," In Cary Y. Liu, Michael Nylan and Anthony Barbieri-Low, *Recarving China's Past: Art, Archaeology, and Architecture of the "Wu Family Shrines,"* edited by Naomi Noble Richard (New Haven and London: Yale University Press, 2005), 439.

[90] Roel Sterckx, *The Animal and the Daemon in Early China* (Albany, NY: State University of New York Press, 2002), 46; also see Ode no. 103 "Lu ling (Here Comes the Hounds)," *Qi feng (Odes of Qi)* and Ode No. 127, "Si tie (Team of Grays)," *Qin feng (Odes of Qin)*. Fu Lipu, *Shijing Mao zhuan yijie* (Taibei: Taiwan shangwu yinshuguan, Minguo 74 [1985]), 362, 439. Translation see Arthur Waley, trans., *The Book of Songs*, edited by Joseph Allen (New York: Grove Press, 1996), 81, 100.

[91] See Virginia Bower, 433-436.

and mythical animals.[92] As we shall see, this imagery has more in common with scenes of the hunt from the Northwest.

The other major motif associated with the hunt in tomb reliefs from this area is an archer aiming at birds or monkeys in a tree. Sometimes this motif occurs by itself[93] or is part of a larger homage scene as in the Wu Liang Shrine (151 CE).[94] The archer appears alongside these scenes more frequently in above ground shrines. This imagery has generated a number of theories that are based on the author's understanding of the figure of the archer, its relationship and frequent inclusion in homage scenes, the tree itself or the animals in the tree.

Traditionally, scholars have identified this scene as illustrating the mythical *fusang* tree and the myth of Archer Yi shooting down the nine renegade suns. Recently, however, many scholars have argued against this interpretation; very rarely are the correct number of birds depicted in the tree and sometimes the birds are joined by monkeys.[95] Xin Lixiang has argued that the archer depicts the filial descendents of the deceased gathering sacrifices while the horse/horse and empty cart that appears in some scenes indicates that the deceased has returned to the shrine to receive offerings.[96] Xing Yitian has argued that the archer aiming at a bird (*she*

---

[92] *Zhonguo huaxiang shi quanji*, Vol. 1, Fig. 160.

[93] *Zhongguo huaxiang shi quanji*, Vol. 3, Fig. 130.

[94] *Zhongguo huaxiang shi quanji*, Vol. 1, Fig. 66.

[95] Cary Y. Liu, "Wu Family Shrines," In Cary Y. Liu, Michael Nylan and Anthony Barbieri-Low, *Recarving China's Past: Art, Archaeology, and Architecture of the "Wu Family Shrines,"* edited by Naomi Noble Richard (New Haven and London: Yale University Press, 2005), 126-127.

[96] Xin Lixaing, *Handai huaxiang shi zonghe yanjiu* (Beijing: Wenwu chubanshe, 2000), 83-102. For a critique of Xin's interpretation see Jiang Yingju, "Handai huaxiang 'louge baiye tu' zhong de dashu fangwei yu zhu tuxiang yiyi (The Direction of Tree and Other Images in the *Louge baiye tu* during the Han Period)," In *Yishu shi yanjiu = The Study of Art History* (Guangzhou: Zhongshan daxue chubanshe, 1999), 149-171. Jiang sides with the interpretation of Xing Yitian. Klaas Ruitenbeek has also identified the archer(s) as the filial descendents of the deceased, but has not argued that these images are part of an extended narrative of the return of the deceased to

*que*) or monkey (*she hou*) are rebuses and shooting at birds represents aiming at a gate pillar (*que*), a sign of high office, while the monkeys are a rebus for noble rank (*hou*).[97] Attempting to fit the figure of the archer into his theory of the tree as representing the Birchleaf pear, Kenneth E. Brashier argues that the archer is instead an accessory figure symbolizing the 'distant wilds' where the Duke of Shao held court.[98] Zhang Congjun has argued that these images refer to stories of a mythical bird who distributes the elixir of immortality made by the jade hare and toad. According to his interpretation, the archers attempt to kill these birds to obtain the coveted elixir.[99] As Patricia Berger has noted, the tree and its associated motifs were multivalant and it is likely that whether included in a tomb or a shrine, scenes of archer(s) shooting at birds/monkeys were part of a web of associated meanings during the Eastern Han dynasty.[100] Berger's reading of this imagery seems the most plausible as it based upon the recognition of the different contexts in which this imagery appeared and the different meanings it could convey.

---

the shrine. Klaas Ruiteenbeek, *Chinese Shadows: Stone Reliefs, Rubbings, and Related Works of Art From the Han Dynasty (206 BC-220 AD)*, 44.

[97] Xing Yitian, "Handai huaxiang zhong de 'Shejue shehou tu' (Eastern Han dynasty Images of Aiming at Nobility and High Rank)," *Bulletin of the Institute of History and Philology*, Vol. 71, No. 1 (2000), 1-66.

[98] This is one of the weakest links in Brashier's interpretation of these scenes which fails to mention the many reliefs that only depict the archer, trees and/or birds and monkeys without the homage scene or horse/empty cart as well as to differentiate which scenes are primarily found in tombs or shrines. Kenneth E. Brashier, "Symbolic Discourse in Eastern Han Memorial Art: The Case of the Birchleaf Pear," *Harvard Journal of Asiatic Studies* 65.2 (2005), 295-299.

[99] Zhang Congjun, "Han huaxiang shi zhong de sheniao tuxiang yu shengxian (Images of Shooting Birds on Han Dynasty Tomb Reliefs and Ascending to Immortality)," *Minsu yanjiu* 2006(3), 152-159.

[100] Patricia Berger is the only scholar who has attempted to explore the many variations of these motifs and connects them to early Chinese mythology and mortuary rituals. Patricia Berger, "Rites and Festivities in the Art of Han China: Shantung and Kiangsu Province," (PhD Dissertation: University of California, Berkeley, 1980), 77-101.

## 3.2     HUNTING IMAGERY IN NANYANG, HENAN

Scenes of the hunt on molded tomb bricks and tomb reliefs from Nanyang, Henan include motifs that we have already seen in Shandong, Jiangsu and Anhui with some regional variations.[101] The archer and tree are more common in tomb bricks than reliefs and they are not combined with homage scenes, but paired with scenes of entertainment.[102] Both hunters and hounds and archers on horseback are common on tomb bricks and reliefs from Nanyang.

The most distinctive imagery related to the hunt in this region are representations of human-animal combat. These scenes decorate the reliefs of door lintels and were popular motifs on molded tomb bricks. In these images, men are paired against a number of animals that include bulls, tigers, bears, monkeys and dragons. A lintel from a tomb in Fangcheng, is typical of this imagery and shows a man fighting two tigers. He wears loose shorts, a pointed hat and has a spear attached to his waist.[103]

Although fights between men and animals are attested to in pre-Han visual and textual sources, it was not until the Western Han dynasty (206 BCE- 8 CE) that such competitions took place on an imperial scale. Tomb reliefs that depict human-animal combat are usually interpreted

---

[101] See Ai Yanding and Li Chenguang for a detailed division of the motifs in this region. Ai Yanding and Li Chenguang, "Shilun Nanyang Handai huaxiang zhong de tianlie huodong (A Discussion of Hunting in Han Dynasty Images from Nanyang)," In *Handai huaxiang shi yanjiu* (Beijing: Wenwu chubanshe, 1986), 219-226.

[102] *Zhongguo huaxiang shi quanji*, Vol. 6, Fig. 97. Such regional variations undermine overarching arguments regarding the significance of the archer and the tree in Han dynasty tomb reliefs. The appearance of this motif alongside scenes of dancers and other performers in Henan suggests that in this region it sometimes simply refers to (informal?) archery competitions held purely for entertainment. In other reliefs, however, this image is joined by a bear and the gods Fu Xi and Nü Gua; such combinations make general interpretations difficult.

[103] Ibid., Fig. 51.

as belonging to a larger category of images associated with the *jiaodi xi* (competitive games).[104]

The origins of the jiaodi xi are obscure, but are thought to have been based upon Shang and Zhou

dynasty (1050-256 BCE) sacrifices and festivals, competitions held during military reviews or on

re-enactments of the battle between Huangdi and Chi You.[105] Regardless of their origins, they

were held a number of times during the Western Han dynasty and included both athletic

competitions and other entertainments such as acrobatics, dancing and plays. Such

entertainments, although briefly suspended in the first century BCE, resumed during the Eastern

Han dynasty and similar activities were sponsored by members of the upper class.[106] Jean M.

James has suggested that such images were placed in tombs to entertain the *po* soul before it

disintegrated and returned and merged with the Earth.[107]

---

[104] See Wang Zijin for a survey of pre-Han textual sources. Wang Zijin, "Handai de dou shou he xunshou (Fighting and Taming Animals during the Han Dynasty)," *Renwen zazhi* 1982(5), 75. See Long Zhong and Sun Shiyan for different divisions of scenes of combat between groups of animals, groups of humans and humans and animals. Long Zhong, "Letan Handai jiaodi xi (A Summary of Han Dynasty Competitive Games)," *Nandu xuetan* 1983(1), 78, 99-100; Sun Shiwen, "Handai jiaodi xi chutan—dui Han huaxiang zhong de jiaodi xi de kaoji (A Preliminary Examination of Han dynasty Competitive Games—Research on Han Images of Competitive Games)," *Dongbei shi daxue ban (zhexue shehui xueban)* 1984(4), 67-71. The only study of these images in English is Richard C. Rudolph, "Bull Grappling in Ancient China," *Archaeology* 13 (1960), 241-245. See also Homer H. Dubs and Mark Edward Lewis for more information on animal combats and the many facets of jiaodi xi. Ban Gu, *History of the Former Han Dynasty*, translated by Homer H. Dubs (Baltimore: Waverly Press, 1954), 2:129-131; Mark Edward Lewis, *Sanctioned Violence in Early China* (Albany, NY: State University of New York Press, 1990), 152-160.

[105] Bo Jian, "Cong jiaodi dao baixi—Qin Han shiqi Zhongguo xiju de yishu zouxiang (From Jiaodi to Baixi—On the Artistic Trend of Chinese Drama in the Period of the Qin and Han dynasties)," *Xuzhou gongcheng xueyuan xuebao*, Vol. 22, No. 2 (May 2007), 5-7; see Michael Loewe for the most detailed accounts of the myth of the battle between Huangdi and Chi You and how it may relate to the jiaodi xi. Michael Loewe, *Divination, Mythology and Monarchy in Han China* (Cambridge: Cambridge University Press, 1994).

[106] Long Zhong, 78.

[107] Jean M. James, "The Role of Nanyang in Han Funerary Iconography," *Oriental Art*, Vol. 36, No. 4 (1990), 223.

From both visual and textual sources we know that the jiaodi xi were strongly associated with Han expansion and the regions and peoples living beyond the Han Empire. Textual sources record that they were often performed for foreign dignitaries and expanded to include a number of entertainments adopted from peoples living in the Western Regions.[108] The association of such activities with non-Han Chinese must have been widespread during the Han dynasty and the figures in scenes of human-animal combat from Henan are shown to be foreigners. This is indicated by their dress and facial characteristics: most figures wear only a pair of billowy pants and a pointed hat and have exaggerated facial features and/or beards that are similar to a "foreign slave (*hu numen*)" depicted with an identifying inscription in a tomb from the same area.[109] Other figures have strange facial features and pointed headgear or hairstyles, both associated with foreigners during the Han dynasty.[110]

---

[108] Bo Jian, 6; See Michael Loewe, *Divination, Mythology and Monarchy in Han China*, 236-23, for an outline of the historical sources which document the circumstances under which the jiaodi xi were performed.

[109] *Zhongguo huaxiang shi quanji*, Vol. 6, Figs. 43 and 44. The physique of these figures and their pants are also very similar to the paunchy wrestlers excavated from the tomb of the First Emperor of Qin.

[110] Rudolph has identified the hairstyle of these figures with characters described in Zhang Heng's "Xi jing fu (Rhapsody on the Western Capital):" "...They send out warriors from Zhonghuang, The peer of Xia Yu and Wu Huo. Wearing vermillion headbands and topknots, Their hair standing as straight as poles, Barechested, brandishing their fists as halberds, with long stides they circle the quarry." "Xijing fu," lines 563-568. *Zhao ming wenxuan yizhu* (Changchun Shi: Jilin wen hi chuban she; Shanghai: Xinhua shudian Shanghai faxing suo faxing, 1988-1994), 100. Translation see Knechtges, trans., 221. Cited in Rudolph, 246. These figures may also be wearing masks supporting the more theatrical interpretations of these scenes; Sun Shiwen, 67-68.

## 3.3     HUNTING IMAGERY IN SICHUAN

Compared to its frequency in other regions, the hunt is not common in tomb reliefs and bricks from Sichuan. The few examples found on molded bricks in the region include archers shooting at birds and/or monkeys in a tree, hunters on foot with hounds in the mountains and mounted archers. Although there are not many images of the hunt from this region, one of the most often reproduced Han dynasty hunting scenes is a tomb brick excavated from Anrenxiang, Dayi, Chengdu, Sichuan that depicts a unique, but common method of hunting in Han and pre-Han China.  The bottom portion of this brick depicts several figures harvesting crops. In the upper register two archers take aim at birds beside a pond/marsh using the *yishe* or the corded-arrow method of hunting.[111]

From the Zhou dynasty through the Eastern Han, corded-arrow hunting was a popular method for catching large birds. Frequently depicted on Eastern Zhou (771-256 BCE) incised and inlaid bronzes, it involved the use of a bow or crossbow with a silk cord attached to a special kind of arrow at one end and a weighted mechanism at the other. In the image from Sichuan, these weights sit on the ground to the left of each of the archers. Corded-arrows were primarily used for large birds such as swan, crane or geese; the line would become wrapped around the neck of the bird and, when the bird flew higher, the weight would then bring it to the ground. These special arrows (with small holes in their tips) have been found in Warring States (475-221

---

[111] *Zhonguo huaxiang zhuan quanji*, Vol. 1 (Chengdu: Sichuan meishu chuban she, 2006), Fig. 109.

BCE) and Han dynasty tombs and several objects from the tomb of Zeng Houyi (c. 433 BCE) may also be paraphernalia used in corded-arrow hunts.[112]

This technique is not found in any Shang dynasty oracle bone inscriptions, but appears in several Eastern Zhou texts. A passage from the *Lüshi chunqiu* (*Mr. Lü's Spring and Autumn Annals*) incudes it among the hunting activites that the "worthy man" uses to sharpen his mind and the *Lunyu* (*The Analects*) states that, Confucius, "子釣而不綱，弋不射宿angled, but did not use a net. He shot but not at birds perching," suggesting that the corded-arrow hunt held a particular place among the leisure activities of the upper class during the Warring States Period.[113] In the "Shi hun li (Ritual of Marriage)" chapter of the *Yi li* (*Rituals and Etiquette*), corded-arrow hunts may also have been associated with weddings: five of the objects that the

---

[112] For more on corded-arrow hunts see Cong Wenjun, "Gudai yishe yu shiren xiushen (The Ancient Corded-Arrow Hunt and the Physical Cultivation of the *Shi*)," *Zhongguo dianji yu wenhua* 1995(04), 35-39; Hsü Chung-shu, "Yishe yu nu zhi suyuan ji guanyu cilei mingwu zhi kaoshi (A Study of the Corded-Arrow Hunt and the Crossbow as well as the Chinese Terms Related to Them)," *Zhongyang yanjiuyuan lishi yan yanjiusuo jikan* (*Bulletin of the Institute of History and Philology, Academica Sinica*), Vol. 4, Part 4 (1932), 417-478; Shen Yongfeng, "Jiang ao jiang xiang yi niao yu yan—tanhua gudai de yishe (Will Soar to Shoot Birds and Geese—a Discussion of Ancient Corded-Arrow Hunting), *Xungen* 2006(5), 80-85; Song Zhaolin, "Zhanguo yishe tu ji yishe suyuan (Warring States Depictions of the Corded-Arrow Hunt and Its Origin)," *Wenwu* 1981(6), 75-77; Zhao Fuxue, "Yishe tan (An Examination of Corded-Arrow Hunting)," *Jiaoyu wenhua daokan* 2008(7), 120-122. For the objects from the tomb of Zeng Houyi see Tan Baiming, "Zeng Houyi mu yishe yongqi chutan—guanyu Zeng Houyi mu chutu jin shutanhuang yu 'anzuo fangchui xing qi' de kaozheng (A Discussion of Articles from the Tomb of Zeng Houyi Used in Corded Arrow Hunting—An Examination Concerning Two Objects Excavated from the Tomb of Zeng Houyi)," *Wenwu* 1993(6), 83-88.
[113] *Lüshi chunqiu* 24/6.2, "Gui Feng (Prizing What is Fitting)." Chen Qiyou, *Lüshi chunqiu xin jiaoshi* (Shanghai: Shanghai guji chubanshe, 2002), 1638. Translation see John Knoblock and Jeffrey Riegel, trans., *The Annals of Lü Buwei* (Stanford: Stanford University Press, 2000), 621-622; *Lunyu*, Chapter 7, Verse 27. Liu Baonan and Gao Liushui, *Lunyu zhengyi* (Taibei: Wenshizhe chubanshe, Minguo 79 [1990]), 276. Burton Watson, trans. *The Analects of Confucius* (New York: Columbia University Press, 2007), 51.

groom gives to the bride/her family were derived from some part of the goose, one of the primary animals caught in corded-arrow hunts.[114]

The association of the corded-arrow hunt as a leisure activity of the aristocracy continued during the Han dynasty and is mentioned in a description of a large imperial hunt in the "Xijing fu (Rhapsody of the Western Capital)." During both the Qin and Han a special official was assigned to coordinate such activities and to care for imperial hunting equipment. It also appears that by the Han dynasty, the popularity of corded-arrow hunts had spread to lower levels of society.[115] Although this method is not frequently depicted in tomb reliefs or bricks it does also appear in a tomb relief from Yangjingangcun, Nanyang, Henan.[116]

## 3.4    HUNTING IMAGERY IN SHAANXI AND SHANXI

These regional variations can be contrasted to scenes of the hunt from the Northwest that are dominated by images of mounted archers on horseback and appear on the lintels of tomb doorways. When compared to the iconography of the hunt in other regions, they are unique in their popularity and the frequency with which they are paired or joined by mythical hybrids and motifs of immortality.[117] Mounted archers accompany chariot processions in the same frieze or adjacent to it. Although the motif of the mounted archer is standardized in this region, hunters on

---

[114] Cong Wenjun, 37; Shen Yongfeng, 84-85; Zhao Fuxue, 121. *Zhou li, Yi li, Li ji* (Yangzhou: Guangling shushe, 2007), 2: 3-6. Translation see John Steele, trans. *The I-li, or Book of Etiquette and Ceremonial* (London, Probsthain & Co. 1917), 18-27.

[115] Zhao Fuxue, 121-122. Ban Gu, "Xijing fu." *Zhao ming Wen xuan zhu yi*, 22. Translation see Knechtges, 137.

[116] Zhao Fuxue, 121-122.

[117] Li Lin, Kang Lanying and Zhao Liguang, 217.

foot with hounds, archers shooting at birds in a tree and human-animal combat are also depicted on some reliefs. Hunters on foot with hounds, however, appear only on one lintel from Suide, Shaanxi[118] and the motif of archers shooting at birds in a tree occurs only on two stones from the same area.[119] This can be compared to reliefs from Shandong, Anhui and Jiangsu, which although not as consistent as scenes from the Northwest, appear to privilege these two motifs over others. The absence of hunting hounds may have been prompted by the natural terrain of the region or it may have been generally uncommon during the Han dynasty for hounds to be used when hunting on horseback. The infrequency of the motif of archers shooting at birds in trees is more difficult to understand because the motif of the tree with a horse beneath it (often accompanied by the archer in Shandong) is not uncommon on tomb doorways in this region.

Scenes of human-animal combat are much more common in the Northwest and decorate several lintels in Suide and Mizhi, Shaanxi. In some of these scenes, these figures are joined by the figure of the mounted archer.[120] As I will argue in Chapter 4, the inclusion of the motif of human-animal combat was probably motivated by the association of such scenes with the Xiongnu, a confederation of nomadic pastoralists, and their customs.

The other characteristic of hunting scenes in the Northwest is that they are often paired or joined by hybrid/mythical animals and motifs associated with immortality, including images of Xiwangmu, hybrid immortals and the fungus of immortality. This can be compared to the

---

[118] Li Guilong and Wang Jianqin, Fig. 3. A few other reliefs do depict creatures that are probably hunting hounds, however, unlike in the reliefs from Shandong, Jiangsu and Anhui these dogs accompany mounted archers; hounds also appear with mounted falconers as well. For examples see *Zhongguo huaxiang shi quanji*, Vol. 5, Figs. 35 and 231.

[119] These can be seen on a relief from the Tomb of Wang Deyuan and another stone from Suide. See Li Guilong and Wang Jianqin, Figs. 41 and 89.

[120] Li Lin, Kang Lanying and Zhao Liguang, 10. Mounted archers may have actually been part of the jiaodi xi as these games were originally developed from both archery and horse riding competitions.

quotidian scenes of the hunt that are common in other regions such as Shandong; although often

lacking vegetation or landscape marker, appear by contrast to take place in the "real" world.

Although some elements of vegetation and landscape imagery in scenes from the Northwest do

appear to depict the geographic and ecological circumstances of the region, more often than not,

hunting scenes in this area occur in a cloud-like landscape, poised presumably between Heaven

and Earth.


## 3.5    GENERAL INTERPRETATIONS OF THE HUNT


Scholars in China, Japan and the U.S. have interpreted scenes of the hunt in Eastern Han

tombs as representations of a pastime of the upper class or connected them to the annual La

festival and offerings of dried meat to the ancestors. Most ignore the variations within hunting

imagery described here, lumping them together into one large category, or providing very similar

analyses when dealing with regional imagery.

Many Chinese scholars have argued that by depicting a leisure activity of the upper class,

hunting scenes reflect the status of the deceased. Such authors loosely connect hunting imagery

in Eastern Han tombs to the aristocratic tradition of the hunt and the grand hunts conducted by

contemporary Han emperors. For these scholars, hunting is also associated with agriculture and

labor/production, with some authors also mentioning its connection to military training.[121]

---

[121] For examples see Wang Jianzhong, *Handai huaxiang shi tonglun* (*A Discussion of Han Dynasty Tomb Reliefs*) (Beijing: Zijin cheng chubanshe, 2001), 415; Yu Weizhao, "Zhongguo huaxiang shi gailun (A General Discussion of Chinese Tomb Reliefs)," In *Zhongguo huaxiang shi quanji* (*Collected Work of Chinese Tomb Reliefs*), Vol. 1, edited by Jiang Yingju (Jinan: Shandong meishu chubanshe, 2000), 14; Zhang Congjun, *Huang He xiayou de Han huaxiang shi*

Inherent in these interpretations is the presumption that such activities were decadent and a sign of the abuse of wealth by the upper class. These interpretations are grounded in Marxist ideology and in the Chinese textual tradition that associates hunting with moral depravity and the fall of kingdoms and dynasties. Hunting was an important marker of social status in ancient China, but these interpretations fail to take into account the complex nature of the hunt as an aristocratic activity and the significance of hunting imagery in a mortuary context.

Jean M. James has also interpreted these scenes as representing the leisure activities of the upper class, but instead of seeing them as passive indicators of social status, she analyzes them in accordance with Han mortuary beliefs. She argues that scenes of the hunt appear in tomb art because it was believed that through their representations the *po* soul could continue to enjoy this activity in the afterlife.[122] Although I do not think her interpretation fits every context, it is grounded in the assumption that these images are not passive representations, but were placed in tombs because it was thought through their depiction the activity could take place in the afterlife.

James also notes that these images refer to the animals captured during hunts and offered as dried meats to the ancestors during the annual La festival.[123] Her interpretation is supported by the fact that the hunt was a major component of ancestral sacrifice in Han and pre-Han China and by comments made by Ying Shao in the *Fengsu tongyi* (*Popular Customs and Traditions*) (c. 250 CE).[124] Doi Yoshiko suggests that scenes of the hunt on the west wall of Eastern Han shrines

---

*yishu* (*Han Dynasty Reliefs from the Lower Reaches of the Yellow River*), Vol. 1 (Jinan: Qi Lu shushe, 2004), 184-186; Zhao Chengkai and Jiang Jishen, *Zoujin Han hua* (*Entering Han Pictures*) (Shanghai: Shanghai shudian chubanshe, 2006), 30-31.

[122] Jean M. James, *A Guide to the Tomb and Shrine Art of the Han Dynasty 206 B.C. to A.D. 220* (Lewiston: The Edwin Mellen Press, 1996), 59.

[123] Ibid.

[124] Ying claimed that the name of the ceremony, La originally meant to hunt (*lie*). See Derek Bodde for a discussion of the possible semantic connections between these terms. Derk Bodde,

depict animals that once captured would be offered to the goddess Xiwangmu as well as the deceased.[125] Xin Lixiang, rejecting Doi's argument suggests that these hunting scenes were chosen to decorate ancestral shrines because of the connection between hunting and ancestral sacrifice.[126] The degree to which either author sees these scenes as active representations that provide offerings for the deceased (or Xiwangmu) is unclear. As I will argue in Chapter 3, the relationship of hunting to ancestor worship is fundamental to understanding the function of scenes of the hunt in Shaanxi and Shanxi, but it was not the only hunting tradition influential in the placement of this imagery in Han tombs.

Wang Zijin has offered an interpretation of some hunting scenes that diverges from previous scholarship arguing that hunting imagery which includes chariot processions and tigers have been misidentified and should be instead understood as scenes that depict tigers attacking travelers. He argues from historical sources that tigers and wolves were a serious obstruction to travel on the main roads throughout the Han Empire. The frequency with which tigers bothered travelers as well as local villagers was viewed as indicative of the state of political affairs and therefore a common trope in political criticism. Wang concludes from this that such imagery represented real events from the life of the deceased, depicted in tombs to commemorate the hardships he survived and to record his bravery.[127]

Wang's study is important in that it reveals how close the wilds remained to even major cities during the Han dynasty. It is also the only work to highlight the connection between

---

*Festivals in Classical China: New Year and Other Annual Observances during the Han Dynasty, 206 B.C.-A.D. 220* (Princeton, NJ: Princeton University Press, 1975), 57-58.

[125] Doi Yoshiko, *Kodai Chūgoku no gazōseki* (Tokyo: Dōhōsha, 1986), 103-111.

[126] Xin Lixiang, 138-139.

[127] Wang Zijin, "Qin Han yidao hu zai—jian zhiyi ji zhong jiu ti 'tianlie' tuxiang mingming (Qin and Han 'Tiger Calamities'—Calling Into Question the Identification of Hunting Images)," *Zhongguo lishi wenwu* 2004(6), 20-27.

hunting imagery and scenes of travel in Han tombs. Unfortunately his final analysis of why such imagery would have been placed in tombs does not emphasize this important connection and, like other Chinese scholars, he argues that it records scenes from daily life. As such he fails to address the important connection between hunting imagery and what I interpret as an attempt to provide protection for the deceased from the dangers that existed beyond the grave.


## 3.6    INTERPRETATIONS OF HUNTING IMAGERY IN THE NORTHWEST

In Chinese scholarship, analyses of hunting imagery in the Northwest is also based on Marxist/Classical interpretations and these scenes are often understood to represent the activities of the deceased, who as a member of the upper class enjoyed the hunt as a form of status-defining decadent entertainment. For example, in *Shanbei Handai huaxiang shi* (*Han Dynasty Tomb Reliefs from Shanbei*), Li Lin, Kang Lanying and Zhao Liguang interpret one scene of the hunt from this region as either: 1) showing the arrogance and complacency of officials enjoying the hunt on horseback, or 2) illustrating those who supported the deceased as a leader, coming to his residence and going out on a hunting expedition.[128] Such interpretations ignore the unique geographic, political and cultural background of the region and the basic distinctiveness of scenes in these tombs.

An earlier article by Kang Lanying provides the most detailed study of hunting scenes from Yulin, Mizhi and Suide, Shaanxi. Rather than focusing on social status and critique, Kang concentrates on the cultural and political background of these images. He divides them into three

---

[128] Li Lin, Kang Lanying and Zhao Liguang, 3-4.

types and briefly outlines the political and social context in which they were made. Kang's study of hunting imagery is unique in Chinese scholarship because he argues that the impetus for placing such images in tombs in this region was not connected to the hunt as a decadent upper class pastime. For him these images reflect the political and social climate of the region and he argues that that the popularity of the hunt in this area resulted from two factors: 1) the significance of the hunt as a form of military training, and 2) the importance of hunting and animal husbandry to the Xiongnu who had intermingled with the Chinese living in the region.[129] These themes have also been stressed in later Chinese scholarship.[130] While I think that these scholars are correct to link the popularity of hunting imagery to the presence of the Xiongnu and the importance of military training in the region, in my view, they do not address the impact of the Xiongnu presence upon the depiction of the afterlife in tombs from the Northwest or the significance of hunting scenes in a mortuary context.

The editors of the archaeological report of the excavations at Dabaodang, Shenmu, Shaanxi, while also stressing the military and cultural significance of the hunt in the region, identify two hunting scenes in these tombs (Tombs M1 and M23) as depictions of the Han general Li Guang (d.119 BCE) hunting tigers. In these scenes, archers on horseback ride left aiming at animals; the last archer in the relief turns and shoots at a roaring tiger. The editors argue that an arrow is lodged in the shoulder of the tiger and identify this archer as Li Guang, a famous general during the Western Han known for victories over the Xiongnu and as a skillful

---

[129] Kang Lanying, "Huaxiang shi suofanying de Shang jun liehou huodong (Hunting Activities in Shang Commandery as Reflected in Tomb Reliefs)," *Wenbo* 1986(3), 48-52.

[130] Lü Jing, "Shanbei Han huaxiang shi tanlun (An Exploration and Discussion of Han Dynasty Tomb Reliefs from Shanbei), *Wenbo* 2004(4), 24-29; Xin Lixiang and Jiang Yingju, 11; Shaanxi sheng kaogu yanjiusuo and Yulin shi wenwu guanli weiyuan hui, eds., *Shenmu Dabaodang: Handai cheng zhi yu mu zang kaogu baogao* (*Shenmu Dabaodang: An Archeological Report of the Remains of a Han Dynasty City and Tombs*) (Beijing: Kexue chubanshe, 2001), 119.

archer. The *Shi ji* records that he killed tigers that were bothering peasants when travelling and contains a strange story of him piercing a tiger-shaped rock with one of his arrows. According to the editors, this is a common theme in tomb reliefs from this region commemorating the bravery of Li.[131]

Based on the iconographical evidence, however, I do not agree with this interpretation. Although images of archers shooting at tigers are found throughout this region, archers also take aim at deer, boar and bears. Within these reliefs there is nothing to suggest that the archer shooting at a tiger should be privileged over others. Instead, this figure, like the other mounted archers, appears to be one of many anonymous hunters, not a local hero.

Shih Hsio-yen, the only scholar who has written at length about reliefs from Shaanxi and Shanxi in English, also stresses the connection between hunting imagery and the Xiongnu, noting the popularity of the motif of the mounted archer with his horse poised in a flying gallop. In her general survey of these reliefs she observes that those who commissioned these images were probably military officials and that this may be a reason for their emphasis on the supernatural over the Confucian or moralizing themes popular in other regions. Shih is unique in pointing out the otherworldly aspect of many of the scenes of the hunt from the Northwest.[132]

---

[131] Shaanxi sheng kaogu yanjiusuo and Yulin shi wenwu guanli weiyuan hui, 118-119. I cannot see the arrow in either the rubbings or photographs of these reliefs, but there is a little bit of red paint trailing down the shoulder of the tigers. For the story of the tiger-shaped rock see *Shi ji* 109, "Li jiangjun liezhuan (The Biography of General Li Guang)." Sima Qian, 2871. Translation see Sima Qian, *Records of the Grand Historian: Han Dynasty II*, 121-122.

[132] Shih, Hsio-yen, "Han Stone Tomb Reliefs from Shensi Province," 58-59, 62; "Early Chinese Pictorial Style: From the Later Han to the Six Dynasties," 126, 130; "Some Fragments from a Han Tomb in the Northwestern Relief Style,"160.

Much of the scholarship on Eastern Han scenes of the hunt assumes that these images reflect real life. Although this makes them informative resources regarding contemporary hunting practices and the life of the deceased, it does not answer why such images would be placed in tombs beyond their authority as status symbols. Although the hunt was clearly associated with the nobility in Han and pre-Han China, it was also connected to a wide variety of concepts beyond aristocratic frivolity and privilege.

In most of the existing scholarship, scenes of the hunt are interpreted as passive imagery. I argue instead that hunting imagery from the Northwest were dynamic representations that were chosen to facilitate the passage of the soul of the deceased. As such, these images were placed in tombs because they were similar to the models of animals and other objects (*mingqi,* spirit/brilliant articles) found in Han tombs that were understood as being both different from and at the same time equivalent to, objects used by the living.[133] Jessica Rawson, arguing against the conception of objects and pictures as mere replicas or models without specific functions, has suggested that objects placed in tombs whether of bronze, pottery or depictions were considered to be equivalent to what they portrayed. As long as the image had the appropriate characteristics, these features gave it the power of what it represented. Realism in the sense of a certain amount of accuracy and completeness was deemed essential in making models and pictures, and the

---

[133] For a review of some of the issues at hand and textual sources regarding mingqi see Cary Y. Liu, "The Concept of 'Brilliant Artifacts' in Han Dynasty Burial Objects and Funerary Architecture: Embodying the Harmony of the Sun and Moon," In *Providing for the Afterlife,* edited by Susan L. Bennington and Cary Y. Liu (New York: China Institute, 2005), 17-29.

entire tomb function. Therefore, according to Rawson, Eastern Han dynasty tomb reliefs decorated tombs to fulfill a specific function in the afterlife.[134]

What sorts of functions might hunting imagery fulfill? In the past, only Jean M. James and Xin Lixiang have argued for a specific role of hunting imagery in tombs and shrines. James argues that the hunt appears in tombs to entertain the *po* soul of the deceased. In Xin's interpretation, the archer represents the filial descendents of the deceased who would continue to gather and offer sacrifices to the deceased in perpetuity.[135] Although both interpretations are likely to be correct in certain contexts, they do not address and cannot explain the strongly regional character of hunting themes and iconography in Han China. I argue that hunting was a popular motif in tombs in the Northwest because these scenes would literally become a part of the afterlife journey of the departed. As such they functioned as dynamic representations that insured the safe passage of the deceased to paradise.

## 3.8    CONCLUSION

In this chapter, I have reviewed the regional characteristics of hunting imagery during the Eastern Han dynasty in order to emphasize the uniqueness of scenes of the hunt from Shaanxi and Shanxi. As I have shown, hunting imagery in this region is distinctive in its standardization of scenes that 1) frequently pair hunting scenes with motifs of immortality and 2) focus on the

---

[134] Jessica Rawson, "The Power of Images: The Model Universe of the First Emperor and its Legacy," *Historical Research*, Vol. 75, No. 188 (May 2002), 123-154.

[135] Of course some of these images decorate above ground shrines where they would have also been viewed by the living. As such the motivations for their creation and their functions would have differed. This does not necessarily mean, however, that such imagery was not to insure the deceased would receive sacrifices as long as the stones remained.

figure of the mounted archer. I have also reviewed previous scholarship relating to the depiction of the hunt in Eastern Han tombs, arguing that it fails to address the regional iconography of the hunt and its multivalent meanings. Most scholarship ignores the fact that such imagery had agency and functioned beyond being mere status symbols or reflections of contemporary life. The motivations behind the iconographic program of the hunt in tombs from the Northwest and its function beyond the grave will be the focus of the following chapters.

**4.0     HUNTING, IMMORTALITY AND THE BORDERLANDS BETWEEN HEAVEN**

**AND EARTH**


In this chapter, I will examine the pairing of quotidian and fantastical hunting scenes with motifs of immortality in tomb reliefs from Shaanxi and Shanxi. Although hunting imagery and motifs of immortality were commonly found in tomb reliefs throughout the Han Empire, it is only in tombs from this region that hybrid *xian* (immortals), the goddess Xiwangmu and other motifs of immortality are combined with scenes of the hunt. In this chapter, I will suggest that the arrangement of these motifs was not random, but an incorporation of two visual and textual traditions that served a distinct function within the tomb. After describing the motifs of immortality that appear in these reliefs, I will concentrate on compositions that include hunting scenes with images of immortals cavorting with birds and beasts. Based on earlier visual and textual traditions, I argue that these motifs were combined in tombs from the Northwest to demarcate, represent and control the perilous region between the world of the living and the dead. I argue that the pacification of animals in both scenes signifies the exorcism of this dangerous region either through the transformation of these animals from ferocious beasts into spirit-guides/helpers or through their death or capture.

In tombs from the Northwest, a limited number of motifs of immortality are combined with hunting scenes. These include: 1) images of the goddess Xiwangmu and/or her consort Dongwanggong, 2) two figures playing the game *liubo*, 3) immortals worshipping a mounded image, 4) *boshan lu* (magic mountain censers), 5) immortals holding out the fungus of immortality (*lingzhi* ; usually imbedded in images with animals but sometimes separate) and 6) immortals and animals frolicking in a stylized landscape. The hunting scenes that are combined with these images include the most popular variations of the hunt in Shaanxi and Shanxi outlined in the preceding chapter: groups of mounted archers, mounted archers and chariot processions, hunters on foot and scenes of human-animal combat.

A set of reliefs excavated from Qingjian, Shaanxi, is representative of the tendency in Shaanxi to combine multiple motifs of immortality with a single hunting scene at the doorway of a tomb.[136] Around the outer section framing these doors are scenes of immortals playing with birds and beasts amid an undulating landscape. The door lintel inside this border is centered on a heavenly horse (*tian ma*), a horned beast (*qilin*) and a dragon. These creatures are flanked by two archers on horseback shooting real animals. Below the lintel on the right and left of the door panels are two stones that depict two pairs of immortals perched atop stylized mushroom-like mountains. The figures on the right are focused on the goddess Xiwangmu and those on the left worship an odd mounded image. Below these two reliefs on either side of the door are two figures with brooms. The addition of a pair of *boshan lu* flanked by two plants that resemble the fungus of immortality in the lower corners of the border also refer to Han dynasty beliefs in

---

[136] Li Lin, Kang Lanying and Zhao Liguang, 217.

immortality. The door panels themselves are decorated with phoenixes, *pushou* monster masks, a tiger and a dragon.

Using the decoration of this door as a guide, I will briefly highlight the significance of four motifs of immortality in this region: the goddess Xiwangmu, immortals worshipping a mounded object, boshan lu and immortals frolicking with animals. As I will show, this last motif was associated with the hunt in tombs from the Northwest, a phenomenon I will examine in the following section.

### 4.1.1 Xiwangmu

The goddess Xiwangmu appears on tomb doorways in the Northwest below hunting scenes directly beneath the lintel on either side of the tomb doors. By the Eastern Han dynasty, Xiwangmu was believed to live on Mount Kunlun and to direct the production of the elixir of immortality. For people of different social backgrounds, Xiwangmu held the keys to happiness in this world and the next and as a result is frequently depicted in Han dynasty tomb art. In reliefs from Shaanxi and Shanxi, she sits atop a tree-like mountain representing the axis-mundi of Mount Kunlun that hovers in mid-air connected to the ground by a thick wavy line. Often this line is flanked by other rocky outcrops where xian and animals perch and with birds that fly towards the deity. Usually a pair of immortals or an immortal and the jade hare pounding the elixir of immortality are depicted on her left and right. Although the goddess is sometimes joined by her consort Dongwanggong, she is most frequently accompanied by two immortals who worship a mounded object or by two figures that play the game *liubo*.

## 4.1.2   Immortals worshipping a mounded object

On the doorway from Qingjian, the figure of Xiwangmu is paired with an image of two immortals who sit atop a tree-like mountain worshiping a mounded object. The immortals face this object in an attidue of service or adoration like those immortals depicted flanking the goddess.   The melting appearance of this object is unparalleled in other Han tomb reliefs, although some elements of the composition are comparable to the depiction of two immortals worshipping a stupa in the Wu Liang Shrine (151 CE).[137]   As Wu Hung has shown, during the Han dynasty a number of Buddhist elements were incorporated in Han imagery and religious thought. As people heard of different aspects of Buddhist doctrine, they saw the Buddha as a foreign deity with powers similar to those of Chinese immortals. Gradually the symbols of the Buddha were conflated with Xiwangmu and Dongwanggong. In funerary art this meant that images of the Buddha were no longer objects of communal worship, but symbols of the desire to obtain immortality after death.[138]

Although the shape of the object in the relief from the Wu Liang Shrine is different from the mounded objects found in tombs in Shaanxi it is also approached by a pair of immortals.  In another relief from Shaanxi paired with Xiwangmu, two immortals appear on either side of a set of small mounds that rise at varying heights forming a figure similar to the Chinese character for mountain, *shan*.[139] Although not identical, this figure bears a closer resemblance to the "stupa" from the Wu Liang Shrine. Since the other images from the Northwest follow the same iconographic format (object flanked by two worshipping immortals) and are paired with

---

[137] *Zhongguo huaxiang shi quanji*, Vol. 1, Fig. 65.

[138] Wu Hung, "Buddhist Elements in Early Chinese Art (2nd and 3rd Centuries AD)," *Artibus Asiae*, Vol. 47, No. 3-4 (1986), 264-273.

[139] *Zhongguo huaxiang shi quanji*, Vol. 5, Fig. 104.

Xiwangmu where Dongwanggong (with whom the Buddha was conflated) should be, it seems that these strange melting objects must represent stupas.

### 4.1.3 *Boshan lu*

Boshan lu are the least commonly depicted motif of immortality in the Northwest. When shown they are always placed in the lower left and right hand corners of the border around tomb doors. Sometimes they are flanked by two vine-like objects that may represent the fungus of immortality as can be seen on the doorway from Qingjian. These objects sit in circular basins. Their decoration includes censers that are unadorned, ones with a few markings that divide the vessel into different registers, or images where their leaf-like decoration accentuates their conical form.

Boshan lu were common burial goods in both the Western and Eastern Han dynasties and were made from a number of different materials including bronze and ceramic. These objects first appeared during the Western Han dynasty, but were based on earlier censers. Their decoration varies from those that are ornamented with space cells which depict animals and humans to censers that are left unadorned. Boshan lu are understood to either represent the Island of Penglai, the immortal paradise in the East China Sea or the western paradise of Mount Kunlun. Although the motif occurs infrequently in the Northwest, the depiction of boshan lu as the main decoration of a stone or register of a stone does not appear in any other region at this time. In Shaanxi, it only occurs in relation to a number of other motifs of immortality and is not found in compositions that do not combine hunting scenes with these motifs.

### 4.1.4   Immortals and Animals in Stylized Landscapes

In addition to the goddess Xiwangmu, the most common motif of immortality found in tombs from the Northwest are images of immortals frolicking with animals in stylized landscapes. Usually these scenes serve as the border for all or part of the outermost layer of decoration that frames the doors of a tomb. They also are found inside around the entranceways to the inner chambers.  The significance of this imagery lies both in the relationship between the immortals and animals depicted in these reliefs and in what these landscapes tell us about conceptions of immortals and the afterlife in Eastern Han China. This imagery was an outgrowth of the fusion of the *yunqi* cloud motif with elements of mountain imagery popular during the Western Han dynasty[140] and was meant suggest both clouds and undulating hills. Arguing from visual and textual traditions, I attribute this imagery to the benevolent and malignant elements of mountain lore in ancient China. As I will show in the following section, elements of this imagery were also adopted by artists when illustrating hunting scenes.

The peculiar, twisting lines from which these animals and immortals dangle, climb and twirl represent the boundary where Heaven and Earth meet. This imagery referred to what was believed to be the abode of immortals during the Eastern Han dynasty: sacred mountains whose towering peaks and ravines floated in and out of the clouds. In Han literature, immortals were believed to live either in the east on the Islands of the Blessed, in the west on Mount Kunlun, or on one the sacred mountains of China, such as Taishan or Huashan.[141] Descriptions of these

---

[140] Kiyohiko Munakata, *Sacred Mountains in Chinese Art* (Urbana, IL: University of Illinois Press, 1991), 20-29.

[141] Huashan and Taishan figure in some mirror inscriptions as well as ballads. For mirror inscriptions see Bernard Kalgren, "Early Chinese Mirror Inscriptions," *Bulletin of the Museum of Far Eastern Antiquities* 6 (1934) and Zhang Jinyi, *Han jing suo fanying de shenhua chuanshuo*

mountains refer to them as the axis-mundi connecting the profane and sacred worlds. In the

*Liezi,* we are given a picture of the Five Islands of the Blessed in the East China Sea:

渤海之東不知幾億萬里，有大壑焉，實惟無底之谷，其下無底…其中有五山
焉：一曰岱輿，二曰員嶠，三曰方壺，四曰瀛洲，五曰蓬萊。其山高下周旋
三萬里，其頂平處九千里。山之中間相去七萬里，以為鄰居焉…所居之人皆
仙聖之種；一日一夕飛相往來者，不可數焉.

> To the East of the Gulf of Chi-li, who knows how many thousands and millions of
> miles, there is a deep ravine, a valley truly without bottom… Within it are five
> mountains, called Tai-yü, Yüan-chiao, Fang-hu, Ying-chou, and P'eng-lai. These
> mountains are thirty thousand miles high, and as many miles round; the tablelands
> on their summits extend for nine thousand miles. It is seventy thousand miles
> from one mountain to the next, but they are considered close neighbors... The men
> who dwell there are all of the race of immortal sages, who fly, too many to be
> counted, to and from one mountain to another in a day and a night. [142]

The Islands of the Blessed figure prominently in stories that highlight the obsessions of

the First Emperor of China (r. 221-206 BCE) and of Han Wudi (r. 140-87 BCE) with

becoming immortal and they seem to have been popular during the Western Han. Mount

Kunlun is described in the *Huainanzi*:

昆侖之丘，或上倍之，是謂涼風之山，登之而不死。或上倍之，是謂懸圃，
登之乃靈，能使風雨。或上倍之，乃維上天，登之乃神…

> If one climbs to a height double that of the Kunlun Mountains, (that peak) is
> called Cool Wind Mountain. If one climbs it, one will not die. If one climbs to a
> height that is doubled again, (that peak) is called Hanging Garden. If one ascends
> it, one will gain supernatural power and be able to control the wind and the rain. If
> one climbs to a height that is doubled yet again, it reaches up to Heaven itself. If
> one mounts to there, one will become a god… [143]

---

*yu shenxian sixiang* (*Mythology and Immortal Thought as Reflected on Han Dynasty Mirrors*)
(Taibei: Guoli Gugong bowuyuan, Minguo 70, 1981), 70-72. For ballads see Anne Birrell,
*Popular Songs and Ballads of Han China* (Honolulu: University Of Hawaii Press, 1993).

[142] *Liezi*, "Tang Wen (The Questions of Tang)." Yan Jie and Yan Beining, *Liezi yi zhu*
(Xianggang Jiulong: Zhonghua shu ju Xianggang fenju, 1987), 115-116. Translation see A.C.
Graham, trans., *The Book of Lieh-tzu* (London: John Murray, 1960), 97.

[143] *Huainanzi* 4, "Zhui xing xun." Liu Wendian, *Huainan honglie jijie* (Taibei: Taiwan shangwu
yin shuguan, Minguo 57 [1968]), 2.4: 5-6. Translation see John S. Major, *Heaven and Earth in
Early Han Thought: Chapters Three, Four, and Five of the "Huainanzi"* (Albany: State

Kunlun is described in other Han texts and was the Western paradise where the goddess Xiwangmu dwelled. By the Eastern Han dynasty, this view of immortal paradise had become the most popular.

Beyond references to sacred mountains as the entrance and/or location of paradise, mountains in ancient China were conceptualized as divine, but treacherous realms. Although more conspicuous in hunting imagery, many of the animals that frequent the stylized landscapes of the immortals in the Northwest are ferocious predators such as tigers, bears, wolves and hybrid beasts. These animals combine with the swirling, sometimes craggy lines to refer to another tradition in ancient China which considered mountains as dangerous realms to be entered at the one's own risk.

Gradually the potentially malignant elements that inhabited mountains were replaced by dead humans who filled official posts in the supernatural bureaucracy (part of the general bureaucratization of the spirit world during the Han dynasty), but originally, most beings that lived on mountains were regarded as dangerous because of their unpredictability, amorality and/or supernatural powers. The *Shanhaijing* describes a number of mountain deities and spirits as monstrous hybrids,[144] that must be ritually pacified. In a later text, the *Baopuzi* (*Master Embracing Simplicity*), Ge Hong (283-343 CE) describes mountains as follows:

> 山無大小，皆有神靈，山大則神大，山小神卽小也。人山而無術，必有患.
> 或被疾病及傷刺，及驚怖不安；或見光影，或聞異聲；或令大木不風而自摧
> 折，巖石無故而自墮落，打擊煞人；或令人述惑狂走，墮落坑谷，或令人遭
> 虎狼毒蟲犯人，　不可經人山也.

---

University of New York Press, 1993), 158. Detailed descriptions and textual analyses of references to Kunlun in the *Huainanzi* and other texts are also included in Major, 150-161.
[144] Terry F. Kleeman, "Mountain Deities in China: The Domestication of the Mountain God and the Subjugation of the Margins," *Journal of the American Oriental Society*, Vol. 114, No. 2 (April-June 1994), 230, 237. Also see Kiyohiko Munakata for a discussion of attitudes toward mountains in ancient China which he describes as a "fear-reverence complex." Munakata, 5.

> All mountains, whether large or small, have gods and spirits. If the mountain is large, the god is great; if the mountain is small, the god is minor. If someone enters the mountain possessed of no magical arts, he will certainly suffer harm. Some will fall victim to acute diseases or be wounded by weapons. When frightened and uneasy, some will see lights and shadows, others will hear strange sounds. Sometimes a huge tree will topple, though there is no wind, or a cliff will collapse for no reason, striking and killing people. Sometimes the man will flee in confusion, tumbling down a cavern or into a gorge; other times he will encounter tigers, wolves, and poisonous insects that attack men. One cannot enter a mountain lightly![145]

The earliest visual counterpart to the representation of mountains as wilderness regions that needed to be physically and spiritually pacified can be found in compositions incised on bronze vessels of the Warring States Period.[146]

I argue that reliefs from the Northwest depicting immortals amid mountainous terrain rely on both the benevolent and malignant elements of mountain lore in ancient China because mountains also suggest the borderlands through which the soul must pass upon death and the capricious and dangerous attributes associated with mountains in ancient China served as a backdrop to the journey of the soul. This dual conception of mountains as representing both the land of immortality and the dangerous lands through which the soul would pass may also be seen on boshan lu popular during the Han dynasty. These objects are usually interpreted as representing Penglai or Kunlun, but a number of them are peopled by figures whose connection to the theme of immortality is unclear. In many tomb reliefs from the Northwest, however, these noxious elements have disappeared from compositions and are replaced by benevolent, felicitous creatures. The exceptions occur when hunting scenes are intermingled with scenes of immortals

---

[145] *Baopuzi* 17, "Deng she (Ascending Mountains and Fording Streams)." Wang Ming, *Baopuzi neipian jiaoshi* (Beijing: Zhonghua shuju, Xinhua shudian, Beijing faxing suo faxing, 1985 [2002 printing]), 299. Translation see Kleeman, 230-231.
[146] Munakata, 12-20.

frolicking with animals. The significance of this will become clearer in what follows, but here I argue that these compositions represent the presence of immortals in mountainous terrain from which hazardous elements have been exorcised.


## 4.2    PATTERNS IN WHICH HUNTING SCENES ARE COMBINED WITH MOTIFS OF IMMORTALITY

Our understanding of the combinations of hunting scenes and motifs of immortality in this region is complicated by the number of lintels excavated in the Northwest that were part of larger unknown compositions. Even with this caveat, a number of patterns emerge based on the inspection of complete and incomplete sets of reliefs. Although many motifs of immortality can be seen on the door described in the introduction from Qingjian, it was far more common for doors to be decorated with only one or two motifs. Usually these included the themes of immortals and animals and the goddess Xiwangmu, but the goddess is sometimes also paired with hunting scenes. The motif of immortals and animals usually decorates tomb reliefs from larger unknown compositions whose horizontal layout suggests that they were door lintels. This strengthens the evidence that exists based on better-preserved reliefs that the theme of immortals frolicking with animals were typically combined with scenes of the hunt. This combination was also common in entranceways between chambers in tombs.

Exceptions to this general pattern can be found in tombs excavated from Dabaodang, Shenmu, Shaanxi. There the motif of immortals and animals is never used as a border for tomb doors, but elements within these reliefs suggest that there was still a strong connection at this site between the stylized landscapes of  immortals and animals and scenes of the hunt. Examples include the lintel of a doorway from Dabaodang Tomb M24 that depicts two foreigners, a *tian ma* (heavenly horse) and an elephant.[147] These figures are placed in the same stylized landscape as scenes that depict immortals cavorting with animals. In another tomb from the same site (M9), a stylized landscape without immortals and animals forms the decorative border of a doorway whose lintel depicts a group of archers on horseback galloping through a landscape that appears to hover in the clouds.[148] Such elements suggest that, although the motif of immortals cavorting with animals appears infrequently in the tomb reliefs from Dabaodang, at this site hunting was also associated with immortality and the borderlands between Heaven and Earth.

In the majority of tombs from the Northwest, the relationship between the motif of immortals frolicking with animals and hunting scenes is more explicit. The clearest connection between these motifs occurs in reliefs where immortals are placed beside or among hunters such as on a stone from Suide, Shaanxi.[149] On the far left stands an immortal holding the fungus of immortality with a tian ma, to the right are archers on horseback and a tiger. Less frequently an immortal or anthropomorphosized animal holding a bow and arrow is depicted with animals in a stylized landscape.[150]

Several of the hunting scenes from Shaanxi also include landscape elements that resemble the stylized landscape of scenes with immortals and animals or have flora that looks like the fungus of immortality. This includes a hunting scene from Guanzhuang Tomb No. 1, Mizhi, Shaanxi, in which the landscape is clearly modeled on the undulating hills of the

---

[147] Shaanxi sheng kaogu yanjiusuo and Yulin shi wenwu guanli weiyuan hui, Fig. 97.
[148] Ibid., Fig. 114.
[149] Li Guilong and Wang Jianqin, Fig. 61b.
[150] *Zhongguo huaxiang shi quanji*, Vol. 5, Fig. 41.

cloudscapes that depict animals and immortals. [151] In other scenes, although the stylized landscape only appears in the border, the flora in the hunting portion is portrayed in the same manner as the fungus of immortality. [152] On still other lintels, the scene of the hunt is framed by a border that resembles the stylized landscape of scenes with immortals and animals. [153]

In the interior of these tombs, the juxtaposition of this imagery also establishes the same connection. In the front chamber of a tomb excavated at Yanjiacha, Suide, Shaanxi, the lintel on the east wall depicts Xiwangmu, Dongwanggong and an entourage leaving what appears to be some sort of complex. [154] They travel through the sky on chariots pulled by dragons, lions, frogs and other animals. The lintel on the west wall depicts a hunting scene with a camel and a large party that leaves a country estate. [155] Below this, on either side of the composition are reliefs which depict a ram and stag. The background for these animals is the same cloudscape found in scenes of immortals and animals. Such imagery demonstrates that the combination of the theme of the hunt with motifs of immortality was carried into the interior of the tomb and used there to create a distinctive landscape of the beyond.

---

[151] Li Lin, Kang Lanying and Zhao Liguang, 8.
[152] Shaanxi sheng kaogu yanjiusuo and Yulin shi wenwu guanli weiyuan hui, Fig. 51.
[153] *Zhongguo huaxiang shi*, Vol. 5, Fig. 207.
[154] Li Guilong and Wang Jianqin, Fig. 24.
[155] Ibid., Fig. 25.

## 4.3    PACIFICATION OF THE BORDERLANDS: IMMORTALS FROLICKING

## WITH ANIMALS AND SCENES OF THE HUNT

These scenes illustrate a regional conception of the afterlife based upon the long-held belief in ancient China that the regions between Heaven and Earth were inhabited by ghosts, malignant spirits and/or capricious ancestors. Our view of the beyond in pre-Han China comes primarily from texts and archaeological materials associated with the state of Chu. Poetic descriptions of the dangerous creatures that awaited the deceased can be found in the *Chu ci* (*Songs of the South*), in the poems, "Zhao hun (Summons of the Soul)" and "Da Zhao (Great Summons)" that describe the work of shamans who attempt to restrain the soul of the deceased from departing or to revive a corpse. Archaeological evidence recovered from Chu tombs has also shown that the structure, funerary goods and texts placed in tombs in this region were believed to facilitate the journey of the deceased to Heaven.[156] As Lai Guolong has argued, these tombs may have been constructed as a sort of way station, motivated by a clear distinction of tame versus wild space.[157] The conception of the region between Heaven and Earth as a perilous wilderness is also suggested by the closing imagery of the "Zhao hun" that describes a solitary hunt in a marshland:[158]

青驪結駟兮，齊千乘.
懸火延起兮，玄顏烝.

---

[156] Constance A. Cook, *Death in Ancient China: The Tale of One Man's Journey* (Brill: Leiden and Boston, 2006); Lai Guolong, "The Baoshan Tomb: Religious Transitions in Art, Ritual, and Text during the Warring States Period (480-221 BCE)," PhD Dissertation, University of California, Los Angeles, 2002.

[157] Lai Guolong, "Death and the Otherworldly Journey in Early China as Seen through Tomb Texts, Travel Paraphernalia and Road Rituals," *Asia Major*, 3rd Series, Vol. 28, Part 1 (2005), 42-43.

[158] Cook, 28-29.

步及驟處兮，誘騁先.
抑鶩若通兮，引車右還.
與王趨夢兮，課後先.
君王親發兮，憚青兕.
朱明承夜兮，時不可以淹.
皋蘭被徑兮，斯路漸.
湛湛江水兮，上有楓.
目極千里兮，傷春心.
魂兮歸來！哀江南！

My team was of four net horses; we set out together a thousand
chariots strong.
The beater's fires flickered skyward, and the smoke rose like a pall.
I trotted to where the throng was, and galloped ahead to draw them,
Then reined as we sighted our quarry, and wheeled around to the
right hand.
I raced with the King in the marshland, to see which of us should
take it.
The King himself shot the arrow; the rhinoceros turned and fled,
'The darkness yields to daylight; we cannot stay much longer.
Marsh orchids cover the path here: this way must be too marshy.'
On, on the river's waters roll; above them grow woods of maple.
The eye travels on a thousand *li*, and the heart breaks for sorrow.
O soul, come back! Alas for the Southern Land![159]

Similar imagery and beliefs are found in Han dynasty tombs, their funerary goods, and in

*zhenmu wen* (tomb-quelling texts):

乙巳日死者鬼名為天光天帝神师已知汝名疾去三千里汝不即南山給口令来食
汝急知律令.

He who died on the i-ssu day has the ghost name "heavenly light" (t'ien kuang).
The Heavenly Emperor and Sacred Teacher already know your name. Quickly go
away 3,000 miles. If you do not go immediately, the (monster?) of the South
Mountain is ordered to eat you. Hurry as prescribed by law and ordinance.[160]

---

[159] Dong Chuping, *Chuci yizhu* (Shanghai: Shanghai guji chubanshe: Xinhua shudian Shanghai
faxing suo faxing, 1986), 265-266. Translation see David Hawks, trans., *The Songs of the South*
(Harmondsworth, Middlesex, England; New York: Penguin Books, 1985), 229-230.
[160] Jiangsu sheng wenwu guanli weiyuan hui,"Jiangsu Kaoyu Shaojiagou Handai yizhi de qingli
(Han Dynasty Remains at Shaojiagou, Jiangsu," *Kaogu* 1960(10), 21. Translation see Poo Mu-
chou, *In Search of Personal Welfare: A View of Ancient Chinese Religion* (Albany, NY: State
University of New York Press, 1998), 174-175.

Han texts more frequently depict an afterlife equipped with a bureaucracy and legal system like that of the ruling government (already present in some Warring States texts) and the recurrent fear that the dead might return and harm the living.[161]

Although the *Chu ci* and Chu tombs are far-removed in both time and space from Eastern Han tombs from the Northwest, imagery within Northwestern tombs also seems to treat the beyond as a dangerous wilderness inhabited by malignant spirits and ferocious beasts. An inscription excavated from a tomb in Suide is similar in style and content to poems from the *Chu ci* complete with Chu style breath marks (兮) and similar imagery of spirits and dangerous animals:

> 哀賢明而不遂兮, 嗟痛淑雅失(?)年. 云日日而下降兮, 荣名絕而不信(申). 精
> 浮遊而猥量獐兮, 魂瑶而東西. 恐精靈而迷惑兮, 歌歸来而自還. 掾兮歸
> 来無妄行, 卒遭毒氣遇匈(凶)殃⋯

> Ah, the enlightened does not follow, oh, the refined has died an early death, he has left the white sun and descended, his honorable name was cut short and not extended. His spirit floats among animals, roaming to the east and west. I am fearful his soul will be confused, I sing for him to return and be restored. Do not go about recklessly, still something poisonous may befall his spirit, and he may encounter misfortune...[162]

This inscription helps to explain the imagery of birds, beasts and hybrids in tombs from Shaanxi and Shanxi, offering a textual record of what the deceased would encounter upon death. I argue that scenes of immortals frolicking with animals and scenes of the hunt in tombs from the Northwest demarcated and symbolized the perilous region described in this inscription. These scenes were meant to symbolize this transitory space, and they were believed to facilitate

---

[161] Poo Mu-chou, *In Search of Personal Welfare*, 171-175.

[162] Translation is mine based on the text provided in Kang Lanying and Wang Zhian, "Shaanxi Suide xian sishilipu huaxiang shi mu diaocha jianbao (A Brief Report on the Tomb Excavated at Sishilipu, Suide, Shaanxi)," *Kaogu yu wenwu* 2002(3), 23.

communication with the beyond by establishing control over these areas. The pacification/control of the animal world in both scenes signifies the exorcism of these hazardous borderlands, either through the transformation of ferocious animals into spirit-guides/helpers or through their death or capture. In the case of immortals, this resulted from the belief in their power over the animal world and their role as shamanistic mediators between Heaven and Earth. The choice of hunting scenes was based on a long association of the hunt with the pacification/exorcism of wilderness regions and the role of the hunt in providing sacrifices for the worship of ancestors and the gods.

### 4.3.1   Immortals and Animals

In the following analysis, I return to scenes of immortals frolicking with animals, arguing that immortals, like divine sages, were believed to have power over animals and they were believed to use this power to exorcise and pacify the dangerous areas between Heaven and Earth. I argue that these scenes represent the transformation of these regions by immortals into a realm where all dangerous elements have been removed. This sage-like power was connected to the role of immortals as shamanistic mediators who, with the aid of animal spirit-guides, guaranteed safe passage for the soul of the deceased. This, combined with the role of immortals as the purveyors of the fungus or elixir of immortality, is the reason for their popularity in tomb reliefs from the Northwest and other regions.

In Shaanxi we find scenes of immortals cavorting with birds and beasts that behave counter to the way in which they would interact naturally, such as for example a tiger playing with deer rather than attacking or consuming them.[163] Scenes of immortals frolicking with

animals appear to act as markers of a world transformed by the power of immortals. From as

early as the Warring States period it was believed that through their virtue and the power of

music, sages and righteous rulers could communicate and manipulate animals' behavior.[164] In

several texts, the ancient sages, Shun and Huangdi, who appear in various myths about the

establishment of the Chinese world order, command and enlist the power of animals.[165] During

the Eastern Han dynasty, Cai Yong (132-192 CE) used similar imagery to symbolize the

harmony between Heaven and man and the ordering of an ideal Confucian world.[166]

Scenes of immortals frolicking with animals also suggest the creatures' role as spirit-

guides for immortals who acted as shamanistic intermediaries between Heaven and Earth.

Shamans and shamanism are concepts that have given rise to many interpretations, but shamans

usually serve as intermediaries between the sacred and profane worlds allowing communities to

to control the unknown and to bring balance to society as a whole.[167] Although in Eastern Han

tomb reliefs immortals do not perform all the functions of shamans, they are depicted as

mediators between the realms of Heaven and Earth who guide the soul of the dead through the

dark spiritual realms of the afterlife. In the Northwest immortals exorcise malignant forces and

transform the realm between Heaven and Earth with the help of animals in ways similar to which

---

[163] *Zhongguo huaxiang shi quanji*, Vol. 5, Fig. 6.

[164] Roel Sterckx, *The Animal and the Daemon, in Early China*, 162.

[165] Mark Edward Lewis, *Flood Myths in Early China* (Albany: State University of New York Press, 2006), 36.

[166] Martin Powers, *Art and Political Expression in Early China* (New Haven: Yale University Press, 1991), 276.

[167] For a review of some of these definitions and approaches to the study of Shamanism see Merete Demant Jakobsen, *Shamanism: Traditional and Contemporary Approaches to the Mastery of Spirits and Healing* (New York: Berghahn Books, 1999), 1-8 and Peter Knecht, "Aspects of Shamanism: An Introduction," in *Shamans in Asia*, eds. Clark Chilson and Peter Knecht (London and New York: Routledge Curzon, 2003), 2-11.

shamans would use their spirit-animals as aids in journeys through spiritual planes. The use of animals as spirit mounts is described in a Han dynasty mirror inscription:

上大山見仙人, 食玉英飲澧泉. 駕交龍乘浮雲. 白虎引兮直上天. 受長命寿萬. 年冝官秩保子孩.

> If you climb Mount T'ai, you may see immortal beings. They feed on the purest jade, they drink from the springs of manna. They yoke the scaly dragons to their carriage, they mount the floating clouds. The white tiger leads them…they ascend straight to heaven.[168]

The role of immortals as intermediaries is also implied by the pictorial arrangement of reliefs where immortals are represented traveling across cloudscapes. Images that depict immortals approaching or ascending mountains in tomb reliefs may also draw on the idea of the ascension/descension of shaman-like figures via an axis-mundi.

Iconographically this imagery in tombs from the Northwest was based on auspicious imagery (*xiangrui*) and the *yunqi* cloud motif that became popular during the Western Han dynasty. These composite motifs were sometimes used to depict hunting scenes as can be seen on a chariot ornament excavated at Sanpanshan, Hebei.[169] Here, birds and animals playfully tumble in a fabulous landscape; both the behavior of the animals and the environment in which they are depicted provide a visual precedent for reliefs which illustrate immortals and animals (as well some scenes of the hunt in tombs from Shaanxi and Shanxi).

Wu Hung has argued that the relationship between the animals and humans on this ornament shows a fundamental change in the emphasis of scenes of the hunt from the Eastern Zhou. Early scenes suggest a more intense sense of conflict between man and beast in which

---

[168] Michael Loewe, *Ways to Paradise*: *The Chinese Quest for Immortality* (London and Boston: Allen & Unwin, 1979), 200.

[169] Zheng Luanming, "Dingzhou Sanpanshan cuo jin yin tong chesan dingxian shi neirong fenxi (An Analysis of the Decoration of an Incised Chariot Ornament from Sanpanshan, Dingzhou)," *Wenwu chunqiu* 2000(3), Fig. 2.

animals are both predator and prey. On the chariot ornament and other scenes of the hunt from the Han dynasty, this sense of urgent combat is lost and the scenes represent an anesthetized, theatrical presentation of the hunt that focuses on the skill and flexibility of the rider and smoothness of the composition. Wu argues that this new harmony resulted from the development of auspicious omen imagery and of the popularity of new beliefs in immortality in which animals served as heavenly envoys bringing good news to mortal men and aiding the dead in their ascension to heaven.[170] The most elaborate expression of such beliefs can be found in scenes from the Northwest which use mountain/cloud and animal imagery to express the unique power of immortals in ordering the animal world.

### 4.3.2  Hunting, Exorcism and Communication with Heaven

Hunting imagery from the Northwest shows a more complex relationship between animals and man than reliefs depicting immortals frolicking with animals. Although some scenes draw on the *xiangrui* tradition of animal and environment as nonthreatening and in agreement, others show that all was not well between the world of animals and the world of man. Rather than playful animals gracing scenes of immortals and animals or anesthetized scenes of the hunt found in other regions during the Eastern Han, animals in the Northwest are depicted as ferocious predators that can and do attack humans. I argue that this tension between animals as helpful mediators and as dangerous predators was an outgrowth of pre-Han and Han dynasty

---

[170] Wu Hung, "Sanpan Shan Chariot Ornament and the Xiangrui Design in Western Han Art," *Archives of Asian Art* 36 (1984), 49-52. For of a discussion of how the motif of the mounted archer in hilly terrain may have been derived from Central Asian nomadic art see Esther Jacobson, "Mountains and Nomads: A Reconsideration of the Origins of Chinese Landscape Representation," *Bulletin of the Museum of Far Eastern Antiquities* 57 (1985), 133-79.

traditions that associated hunting and archery with exorcism and ancestral sacrifice. The contradictory representation of animals within these reliefs was based on a desire to equate the beyond, illustrated in scenes of immortals frolicking with animals, with scenes of the hunt while continuing to view animals as dangerous and as symbolic of the hazards that the deceased would encounter. Although the relationship between man and animal in scenes of immortals frolicking with birds and beasts and in hunting imagery is different, both were meant to exorcize the spiritual borderlands of the afterlife and establish communication between Heaven and Earth through control over the animal world.

### 4.3.3   The Relationship between Animals and Man in Scenes of the Hunt from the Northwest

To judge from the relationship between man and animals in tombs from the Northwest, scenes of the hunt can be divided into two categories: 1) scenes in which animals are portrayed within the xiangrui tradition, often including immortals or the fungus of immortality in the same relief, or 2) scenes in which the hunt is portrayed "realistically" or where animals are depicted as either predator and prey. Scenes which are an outgrowth of the xiangrui imagery mix auspicious animal imagery with scenes in which animals appear to walk playfully toward hunters such as on a lintel from Sishipu, Suide, Shaanxi.[171] In this relief, a boar, deer, tiger and another animal walk toward two hunters, one with drawn bow and another who is about to release a hound. On the far left a mythical plant, qilin and phoenix are also included in the composition. In other reliefs, hunters and animals are separated by vegetation reminiscent of the fungus of immortality and

---

[171] Li Guilong and Wang Jianqin, Fig. 3.

sometimes joined by immortals or other magical animals. In one relief from Mizhi, a tiger, which reappears in many hunting scenes looks like it is wagging its tail as two archers take aim to its right.[172] This tiger also can be seen in reliefs with fabulous/auspicious animals that parade across tomb lintels.

This "happy" tiger can be compared to the tigers on the lintel of the doorway to Guanzhong Tomb No. 2, Mizhi, Shaanxi.[173] In this relief, three men on foot attack and are hunted by tigers. One of these tigers bites the foot of a man holding an ax; another pounces on the leg of an archer as he draws back his bow. In another stone excavated from Mizhi, mounted hunters use bows and arrows or lances to hunt animals, several of which turn to assault their attackers. To these types of images can be added more realistic hunting scenes such as the one found in the Yanjiacha tomb in Suide that depicts a party leaving an estate and travelling into the wilderness on a hunt.[174]

These reliefs do not depict the harmonious universe of xiangrui imagery, but a world in which man engages in intense combat with ferocious animals. The inclusion of such scenes, sometimes juxtaposed with xiangrui imagery and motifs of immortality, drew upon hunting traditions that associated it with exorcism/pacification of the wilderness and communication with the spirit world through ancestral sacrifice.

The earliest rendering of the hunt as an exorcistic ritual to open up communication with Heaven is found in hunting scenes on Warring States pictorial bronze vessels. These provide the first examples of pictorial representation in early Chinese art and are the earliest extent precursors to Han dynasty hunting imagery. Although the forms of these vessels were derived

---

[172] Li Lin, Kang Lanying and Zhao Liguang, 35, Fig. 117.
[173] Ibid., 12.
[174] Li Guilong and Wang Jianqin, Fig. 25.

from those used in ancestor worship, many were probably made as personal objects to be used by the aristocratic class.[175] These vessels have been studied by scholars in China, Japan and the West, but many questions remain regarding their production, the origin of their imagery and their sudden and brief appearance in the archaeological record.[176]

The scenes of hunting and human-animal combat on these vessels are the earliest scenes of the hunt to show the demarcation and pacification of the realms between Heaven and Earth. This imagery can be seen on fragments of an incised vessel from a tomb in Gaozhuang, Jiangsu that shows a mountainous landscape filled with animals and multi-headed hybrids.[177] In the first fragment, a number of hunters, including one with a bird-like head, are shown among a profusion of birds and animals. The area of decoration above this scene is filled with tigers, birds, other animals and hybrid creatures depicted among trees and mountainous forms. Another fragment illustrates a figure on a chariot that is surrounded by animals; a number of figures proceed in front of him on foot carrying weapons. Basing his interpretation on the dragon-like character of the chariot and the absence of an archer who is standard in other Warring States chariot hunting scenes, Kiyohiko Munakata identifies this scene as the journey of the soul of the deceased or perhaps the coveyance of a royal messenger to Heaven, both through a wilderness.[178]

---

[175] Mary C. Fong, "The Origin of the Chinese Representation of the Human Figure," *Artibus Asiae*, Vol. 49, No. 1 (1988-89), 6-7.

[176] See Esther Jacobson and Alain Thote for synopsis of the different approaches taken by Chinese, Japanese and Western scholars. Esther Jacobson, "The Structure of Narrative in Early Chinese Pictorial Vessels," *Representations* 8 (Autumn 1984), 61-62; Alain Thote, "Intercultural Relations as Seen from Chinese Pictorial Bronzes of the Fifth Century, B.C.E.," *Res* 35 (Spring 1999), 14.

[177] Huaiyinshi bowuguan, "Huaiyin Gaozhuang Zhanguo mu (A Warring States Tomb from Gaozhuang, Huaiyin)," *Kaogu xuebao* 1988(2), Fig. 25.

[178] Munakata, 15.

Similar scenes appear on other vessels. A *dou* excavated from Pingshan, Hebei and a *hu* from the Gaowangsi hoard include scenes of semi-clad figures with swords, lances, nets and bows. On the dou, this scene decorates the belly of the main container and on the hu, this motif is depicted on the lowest register.[179] Imagery on a "hunting hu" excavated from a tomb at Liulige, Henan, supports the connection between hunting and exorcism.[180] On this vessel, scenes of human-animal combat are paired with images of birds grasping snakes, hybrid bird figures with serpent/dragon-like animals, and winged humanoids grasping snakes that resemble the images found on the incised fragments from the tomb at Gaozhuang. As Munakata has argued, elements of this imagery are symbolic of shamanic ascension (hybrid winged figures) and the exorcism of wilderness regions (birds/humans grasping snakes). Human-animal combat is illustrated on the third and fourth register of the vessel where one figure (with a tail?) faces a huge leopard and another two figures battle a bull-like animal with a long horn (*si*). When these figures and motifs are combined and compared with other humanoids in hunting scenes on pictorial bronzes, it becomes clear that these vessels do not depict quotidian hunting scenes. To judge from the winged figure (second register from the top) on the *hu*, the figure in the chariot and from similar winged creatures on the fragments from Gaozhuang, they seem to represent heavenly/helper spirits who are pacifying the borderlands through which a spirit ascends.[181] Therefore, some hunting scenes on pictorial bronzes were meant to symbolize the pacification of the borderlands through which a figure passed, whether the figure was acting as a shaman or the spirit of the deceased.

---

[179] Han Wei and Cao Mingtan, "Shaanxi Fengxiang Gaowangsi Zhanguo tongqi jiaozang (A Warring States Bronze Hoard from Gaowangsi, Fengxiang, Shaanxi)," *Wenwu* 1981(1), Plate 6:4.
[180] Guo Baojun, *Shanbiaozhen yu Liulige* (Beijing: Kexue chubanshe, 1959), Plate 93.
[181] Munakata, 14-19.

Although many pictorial bronzes contain these motifs, others depict quotidian scenes of aristocratic life that include corded-arrow hunts, chariot hunts and archery contests. Based on passages from the *Zuo Zhuan* (*Chronicle of Zuo*) and the *Zhou li* (*Rites of Zhou*), Roel Stercx has suggested that the hunting of animals in the wild was a prerogative of the aristocracy during the Eastern Zhou (770-221 BCE)[182] and visual and textual evidence demonstrate that corded-arrow hunts, chariot hunts and archery contests were integral to aristocratic life. Although these scenes refer to hunting/archery contests as they would have been practiced, they are also spiritually-charged illustrations that refer to the exorcistic qualities of the hunt and/or the importance of hunting to the ancestral sacrifices that were the foundation of Zhou feudal society.

Based on archaeological and textual evidence, from the Shang dynasty through the Warring States period, chariot hunting was the most glorified form of the aristocratic hunt and was connected with warfare and ancestral sacrifice. Chen Pan was the first to argue that, as early as the Shang dynasty (c. 1500-1046 BCE), hunting was connected with royal ancestor worship both out of a practical need for sacrificial offerings and as a demonstration of respect and devotion.[183] More recently Elizabeth Childs-Johnson has argued that the Shang dynasty *taotie* symbolized the four major animals (buffalo, deer, wild sheep and tiger) that were hunted by the Shang ruler for use in sacrifices to the ancestors and the other high gods.[184] These views have

---

[182] Roel Sterckx, "Attitudes toward Wildlife and the Hunt in Pre-Buddhist China," In *Wildlife in Asia: Cultural Perspectives*, ed. John Knight (London: Routledge/Curzon, 2004), 22.

[183] Chen Pan, "Gu shehui tianshou yu jisi zhi guanxi (The Relationship Between Hunting and Ritual Sacrifice in the Society of Ancient China)," *Zhongyang yanjiuyuan lishi yan yanjiusuo jikan* (*Bulletin of the Institute of History and Philology, Academica Sinica*), Vol. 21, Part 1 (1949), 1-17.

[184] Elizabeth Childs-Johnson, "The Demon Who Devours but Cannot Swallow: Human to Animal Metamorphosis in Shang Ritual Bronze Imagery," In *Chinese Archaeology Enters the Twenty-First Century Symposium Papers*, edited by Beijing University Department of Archaeology (Beijing: Beijing University Press, 1995).

been rejected by Magnus Fiskesjö, who argues from archaeological evidence and oracle bone inscriptions, that wild animals, including deer, were rarely sacrificed during the Shang dynasty. Rather than seeing hunts as tied to the maintenance of the ancestral cult, Fiskesjö envisions the Shang monarch as a "hunter-king" ruling over an agricultural society where the capture of wild animals was a form of symbolic risk taking used by rulers to affirm their power.[185]

The exact relationship between Shang hunting and ancestor sacrifice demands further study, but it is clear that by the Shang dynasty, meat and wine served in bronze vessels was the medium of communication with the spirit world. This provided one of the most important motivations for the emphasis placed on hunt by the Zhou king and the succeeding Warring States aristocracy. During this long period, rulership was based on the worship of powerful ancestral spirits and regional deities through sacrifices made at ancestral and state temples. Hunting was intricately tied to these ceremonies because it provided meat for offerings and because of its close association with warfare which according to the *Zuo Zhuan* was one of the two "great services" of the state. Hunts were also elements of rituals in major sacrifices.[186] Although people in pre-Han China used domesticated animals in some sacrifices, it may have been believed, as Lü

---

[185] Fiskesjö notes that wild animals have only been found in royal tombs and several sacrificial pits in the royal cemetery at Anyang; domestic animals dominate these areas as well. Fiskesjö argues that the Shang preference for domestic animals in sacrifice is because wild animals could not be domesticated and incorporated into Shang culture and were thus deemed unsuitable for sacrificial use. What exactly happened to the wild animals captured or killed on the Shang king's hunt remains unclear, partially as a result of the lack of precise archaeological records for earlier excavations and lack of attention to such issues. Further complicating the picture is the precise nature of the bovine remains found at Anyang and whether these animals were wild or domesticated. Magnus Fiskesjö, "Rising from Blood-stained Fields: Royal Hunting and State Formation in Shang China," *Bulletin of the Museum of Far Eastern Antiquities* 73 (2001), 143-144, 146-149, 152-156.

[186] Lewis, *Sanctioned Violence in Early China*, 17, 21; *Zuo Zhuan*, Lord Cheng, year 13. Yang Bojun, *Chunqiu Zuo Zhuan* (Beijing: Zhonghua. 1981), 861.

Simian has suggested, that wild animals were considered more appropriate as sacrificial offerings because they were "natural" and had not been raised by man.[187]

Western Zhou (1046-771 BCE) bronze inscriptions, poems from the *Shi jing* (*Book of Odes*), and later passages from the "Stone Drum" inscriptions demonstrate the importance of large scale hunting as a way of providing sacrificial animals for temples. The connection between hunting and sacrifice is also stressed by the *Li ji* (*Book of Rites*) and the *Zhou li*, two ritual manuals that were compiled during the Han dynasty. Both mention the need for seasonal hunting to provide animals for sacrifices and refer to officials who prepared game for use in ancestor worship and other temple rituals.[188]

Such practives were adopted and expanded in later Qin and Han imperial parks whose ritualized hunts are described in later texts.[189] The "Liyi zhi (Treatise on Ritual)" in the *Hou Han shu* (*History of the Latter Han*) provides a detailed account of a hunt that was part of the Quliu sacrifice held annually in the fall probably in an imperial park:[190]

> 立秋之日，自郊禮畢，始揚威武，斬牲於郊東門，以薦陵廟. 其儀：乘輿御
> 戎路，白馬朱鬣，躬執弩射牲. 牲以鹿麛. 太宰令、謁者各一人，載獲車，馳
> 馹送陵廟. 還宮，遣使者齎束帛以賜武官. 武官肄兵，習戰陣之儀、斬牲之，
> 名曰貙劉.

> On the day of Autumn's Beginning, with the completion of the suburban ceremony, severity and martial vigor begin to flourish. Animal victims are slaughtered at the suburban eastern gate so that they may be offered in the temples of the imperial tombs. In this ceremony, the emperor rides in a war chariot of white horses, with deep red manes. He himself holds a crossbow in his hands which he shoots the sacrificial victims. These victims consist of young deer. The

---

[187] Lü Simian, *Xian Qin Shi* (*Pre-Qin History*) (Shanghai: Shanghai guji chubanshe: Xinhua shudian Shanghai faxing suo faxing, 1982), 305-306; Cited in Huang Linbin, "Zhoudai liehou wenhua shulüe (A Summary of Zhou Dynasty Hunting Culture)," *Wenshi zazhi* 2000 (2), 41.

[188] Lewis, *Sanctioned Violence in Early China*, 17, 22, 21.

[189] Ibid., 20, 23-24.

[190] See Derk Bodde for a discussion of where this ritual may have taken place, Derk Bodde, 331-332.

Perfect Grand Butcher and Internuncios load the game in chariots and drive them to the imperial tombs, one man for each [tomb]. Then the Emperor returns to the palace. Messengers are sent to give bundles of silk as presents to the military officers, who drill the troops in military formations. The ceremony of slaughtering the sacrificial victims is known as the Ch'u-liu. [191]

A passage from the "Jisi zhi (Treatise on Sacrifice)" from the *Hou Han shu* clarifies that the slaughtered animals were also sent to the imperial ancestral temple in the capital[192] suggesting that during the Han dynasty, the hunt continued to be connected with ancestral sacrifice and with communication with Heaven.

Archery contests were also part of the tradition of the hunt in Zhou China and were connected to ancestor worship and the pacification of animals and the wilderness. Scenes of archery contests are a dominant motif on pictorial bronzes because archery was connected to ritual, social position, masculinity, and moral virtue.[193] Here I wish to highlight the importance of the hunt to the Warring States aristocracy, its relationship to ancestor worship and its connection to pacification/exorcism through the use of skins of wild animals as targets.

During the Warring States period, the practice of archery was a prerogative of the aristocracy, defining a person's position within the social, political and ritual hierarchy. According to the *Li ji*, archery competitions were held to test prospective officials and were the means by which Zhou kings chose who would join them in state rituals, including ancestral

---

[191] Ibid., 327-328. Fan Ye, 3123.

[192] Derk Bodde, 329. Fan Ye, 3182. See Bodde for a detailed analysis of textual references to this Quliu sacrifice, 332-339.

[193] *Wenwu* 1976(3), Plate 2. The connection between virtue (and physical beauty) with the skill of archery is clearly expressed in Ode No. 106 ("Yi jie (Hey ho!)," Qi feng (Odes of Qi). Fu Lipu, 371. Translation see Waley, 82-83.

sacrifices. Archery contests were also held by the rulers of other states, during state visits, and as *yan she*, a type of entertainment at the end of a state banquet.[194]

In addition to affirming the social hierarchy and their connections to ancestor worship, archery contests had exorcistic overtones. A passage from the *Zhou li* describes the construction and function of the targets used in archery rituals, connecting their construction and archery to the submission of other states. Based on commentary by Zheng Xuan (127-200 CE) and other Han texts, these targets were made in the shape of men and covered with animal skins.[195] A detailed description of these animal skins is given in the *Yi li* (*Ceremonies and Rituals*):

> 天子熊侯，白質；諸侯麋侯，赤質；大夫布侯，畫以虎豹；士布侯，畫以鹿 豕.

> As for targets, the Son of Heaven's target has a (picture) of a bear's (head) on a white background; the feudal lord has a tailed deer target on a red background, with (the heads) of a tiger and a leopard drawn on it; the ordinary officer a cloth target, with (the heads of) a deer and a wild boar drawn on it.[196]

As Roel Sterckx has noted, the text implies that the marksmen were believed to be given the controlling or exorcising power of the animal identified on their target. In the case of the Son of Heaven, this included power over "malcontents--" unsubmissive barbarians and unruly vassals whom the ruler ritually pacified by transforming the animal targets into such figures.[197] This interpretation is further supported by comments made by the Eastern Han social critic, Wang Chong (27-100 CE) who understood the symbolism of this ritual to be the subjugation of the

---

[194] Fong, 11.

[195] See Jeffrey Riegel for a detailed discussion of these textual passages and their terminology. Jeffrey K. Riegel, "Early Chinese Target Magic," *Journal of Chinese Religions* 10 (Fall 1982), 2.

[196] *Zhou li, Yi li, Li ji*, 2:19-20. Translation see Roel Sterckx, "Attitudes toward the Hunt in Pre-Buddhist China," 22.

[197] Roel Sterckx, "Attitudes toward the Hunt in Pre-Buddhist China," 23; Riegel, 3-4.

wilds and unruly vassals.[198] This sympathetic magic extended to other participants in archery

contests and the *Baihutong* (*Discussions in the White Tiger Hall*, 78 CE) and *Shuowen jiezi*

(*Explaining Simple and Analyzing Compound Characters*, early 2nd c. CE) both mention that the

*shi* (gentlemen) shot animal targets to drive out evil from the fields. The exorcistic and magical

qualities of skilled archers are also referred to in Ode No. 25 ("Zuo Yu," *Shao Nan* [*Odes of*

*Shao*]) in which an archer discharges one arrow while hunting five boars.[199] Other associations

between exorcism and archery in Han times can be found in descriptions of the Da nuo (Grand

Exorcism) and in the medical manuscripts from Mawangdui Tomb No. 3 which includes the

shooting of arrows among its many cures for inguinal swelling.[200] Visually, archery is also

connected to exorcistic rituals depicted on objects such as a Warring States zither that depicts a

shamanistic figure drawing a bow and the black lacquer coffin from Mawangdui Tomb No. 1 (c.

168 BCE) is decorated with goat-like and vulpine figures that shoot at birds and beasts. These

two funerary goods provide evdince of a strong connection between archery, exorcism and the

protection of the deceased in a mortuary context.

---

[198] *Lunheng* 16, "Luan long (A Last Word on Dragons)." Wang Chong, 248. Translation see
Alfred Forke, 2: 355-356.

[199] See Roel Sterckx, "Attitudes toward the Hunt in Pre-Buddhist China," 23; and Riegel, 3-4 for
discussions of the multiple textual passages and commentaries which discuss these archery
contests. Ban Gu, *Baihutong shu zheng*. Annotated by Chen Li and Wu Zeyu, (Beijing:
Zhonghua shu ju, 1994), 243. Translation see Ban Gu, *Po hu T'ung: The Comprehensive
Discussions in the White Tiger Hall*, translated by Tjan Tjoe Som (Leiden: E. J. Brill, 1949), 2:
474-475; Xu Shen, *Shuo wen jiezi* entry for "hou," 3924; Fu Lipu,133. Translation see Waley,
22.

[200] Based on a description of the Da Nuo in Zhang Heng's "Dongjing fu." *Zhao ming wen xuan
zhuyi*, 164. Translation see David R. Knechtges, trans. *Wen Xuan or Reflections of Refined
Literature*, 1: 291-297; Donald J. Harper, *Early Chinese Medical Literature: the Mawangdui
Medical Manuscripts* (London; New York: Kegan Paul International; New York: Columbia
University Press, 1998), 169, 265 (*MSI.E.132*; *MSI.E.137*). Cited in Riegel, 10, fn. 1.

## 4.4    CONCLUSION

In this chapter I have argued that the pairing of immortality and hunting motifs in tombs from the Northwest formed a set of complimentary representations depicting and facilitating the journey of the deceased. In these tombs, scenes of immortals frolicking with animals signified the sage-like power of immortals who functioned as intermediaries between Heaven and Earth, protecting and guiding the soul on its journey to paradise. Scenes of the hunt offered a complimentary vision of the beyond by providing a means of overcoming these obstacles either by "cleansing" the wilderness through which the deceased must pass, or by enabling communication with the beyond through the offerings of slain animals as sacrifice. This hunting imagery was based on visual and textual traditions of the hunt in pre-Han China that associated it with exorcism and ancestral sacrifice.

Within these tombs this imagery is found on doorways and entranceways between tomb chambers, significant architectural points of disjunction between the world of the living and that of the dead. Immortal imagery and scenes of the hunt were placed at these points to remind the living of what lay beyond the grave and to facilitate the safe passage of the departed to a less dangerous realm. Based on the presence of the goddess Xiwangmu in tomb reliefs from this region, it seems likely that, after a dangerous journey aided by immortals and hunters, the deceased was expected to arrive in her Western paradise. Scenes of immortals frolicking with animals and the hunt represented and facilitated the passage of the soul to this heavenly realm.

# 5.0 "THE PEOPLE WHO LIVE BY DRAWING THE BOW" AND REPRESENTATIONS OF THE AFTERLIFE IN HUNTING IMAGERY FROM THE NORTHWEST

In the previous chapter I have shown that hunting imagery in the Northwest is paired with motifs of immortality to combat a dangerous and fluctuating vision of the afterlife. In this chapter, I argue that this world is ultimately the domain of the mounted archer who, through his hunting, destroys the ferocious animals, malignant spirits and other dangers that threaten the deceased. During the Han dynasty, the figure of the mounted archer was associated with the Xiongnu, "引弓之民 the people who live by drawing the bow,"[201] along with falconry and animal-human combat, activities that are represented in hunting scenes from this region. I suggest that the representation of these "foreign" activities was part of a regional view of the afterlife that equated the borderlands through which the deceased must pass with the world of the Xiongnu. This connection was based on Han dynasty perceptions of the Xiongnu domains as a barren wilderness and of the Xiongnu themselves, who for much of the Han dynasty remained the quintessential barbarian enemy to the Han Chinese. I argue that the military might of the Xiongnu, together with their status as outsiders, made them powerful figures who were believed to be capable of either thwarting or aiding the deceased in the afterlife. These two conceptions

---

[201] As opposed to the Chinese, who, "冠帶 wear caps and girdles." See *Shi ji* 110, "Xiongnu liezhuan (Account of the Xiongnu)."

of the Xiongnu and their world lie behind the popularity of mounted archers in hunting scenes in Shaanxi and Shanxi.

In order to understand the complex nature of this imagery, I will first establish the connection between the Xiongnu and representations of mounted archers, falconry and human-animal combat in tomb reliefs from the Northwest. Highlighting the martial nature of this imagery, I will then focus on the relationship between the figure of the mounted archer, traditional Chinese associations of hunting with warfare, and changing conceptions of the ideal warrior during the Han dynasty. Following this I turn to Han textual descriptions of the Xiongnu and the Northern Steppe, demonstrating their affinities with the landscape and inhabitants of the borderlands between Heaven and Earth. Finally, I will look at depictions of foreigners in Eastern Han tombs to demonstrate how foreigners, as political and cultural outsiders, were suggested to be both benevolent and malignant denizens of the afterlife. I conclude that, in Eastern Han tombs from the Northwest, the Xiongnu in death, as in life, were characterized as ambiguous figures, as both friend and foe to the patrons of these images.


## 5.1    THE FIGURE OF THE MOUNTED ARCHER


Hunting scenes from the Northwest are dominated by the figure of the mounted archer who appears alone, in groups, or within chariot processions. In some scenes, mounted hunters use other weapons such as spears or swords, but this is less common. Unlike Western Han mounted archers that are depicted with a mixture of Han and non-Han attributes,[202] most mounted archers in the Northwest are clearly presented as Han Chinese. As I will show, however, these figures are still engaged in an activity that was strongly associated with the Xiongnu, "the people who live by drawing the bow."

The earliest appearances of the mounted archer are found on a third century BCE hunting scene on a Qin dynasty (221-206 BCE) brick and a mural from Palace No. 3 at the Qin capital of Xianyang.[203] During the Western Han dynasty the popularity of the mounted archer grew, eclipsing scenes of chariot hunting, corded-arrow hunts and archery contests that had been common throughout most of China during the Warring States period. Throughout the first and second centuries BCE it remained a popular motif and was represented on chariot ornaments, hill jars, lacquerware and tomb bricks.

The sudden appearance and popularity of the mounted archer has generated a number of theories regarding its origins all of which agree that such imagery was not native to China. Esther Jacobson has argued most convincingly that it was adopted and adapted from Scytho-Siberian material culture. As she has shown, this motif was associated from the beginning with the nomadic lifestyle and material culture of those living to the north of central China.[204]

------

[202] Zheng Luanming, "Dingzhou Sanpanshan cuo jin yin tong chesan dingxian shi neirong fenxi (An Analysis of the Decoration of an Incised Chariot Ornament from Sanpanshan, Dingzhou)," *Wenwu chunqiu* 2000(3), Fig. 2.

[203] For the brick see Li Jian, ed., *Eternal China: Splendors from the First Dynasties* (Dayton, OH: Dayton Art Institute, 1998), 98; for the palace mural see Shanxi sheng kaogu yanjiusuo, *Qin du Xianyang kaogu baogao* (*The Archaeological Report of the Qin Capital of Xianyang*) (Beijing: Kexue chubanshe, 2004), Image 12.1.

[204] Esther Jacobson, "Mountains and Nomads: A Reconsideration of the Origins of Chinese Landscape Representation," 133-179. Berthold Laufer has argued for similar origins of this imagery in *Chinese Pottery of the Han Dynasty*, 2nd Edition (Rutland, VE and Tokyo: C.E. Tuttle Co., 1962), 212-222. Alexander Soper and Michael Sullivan have both claimed that the figure of the mounted archer and later Sassanid (226-651 CE) hunting scenes were descended from "lost"

During the Warring States period contact with northern nomadic groups intensified as individual states sought to push their borders northward. This contact resulted in a growing interest in foreign customs and exotic material culture. During this time mounted archery and nomadic costume were introduced by royal decree in the state of Zhao in 307 BCE, in an attempt to conquer neighboring non-Chinese and Chinese states.[205] Due to pressures from Chinese expansion and internal development, these groups of people eventually joined forces to form the Xiongnu Empire in the third century BCE. Contact and conflict intensified between the Xiongnu and Chinese with the founding of the Qin and Han Empires and the expansion of Xiongnu power.

Although during much of the Han dynasty the Xiongnu were to remain the greatest real and perceived enemy of the Han Empire, historic records profess to the introduction and popularity of Xiongnu exotica that flowed into the Han Empire as gifts received from Xiongnu delegations and what must have been extensive trading:[206]

夫中國一端之縵, 得匈奴累金之物... 是以騾驢馲駝，銜尾入塞，騨騱騵馬，
盡為我畜，鼲貂狐貉，采旃文罽，充於內府…是則外國之物內流...

Thus a piece of silk can be exchanged with the Hsiung-nu for articles worth
several pieces of gold...Mules, donkey and camels enter the frontier in unbroken
lines; horses, dapples, and bays and prancing mounts, come into our possession.

---

Achaemenian (550-330 BCE) hunting scenes. Such scenes are still waiting to be discovered. Alexander Soper, "Early Chinese Landscape Painting," *Art Bulletin* 23.2 (June 1941), 147; "On the Origin of Landscape Representation in Chinese Art," *Archives of the Chinese Art Society of America* 7 (1953), 54-65; Michael Sullivan, *The Birth of Landscape Painting in China* (Berkeley: University of California Press, 1962), 43-46.
[205] *Shi ji* 43, "Zhao shijia (The Ruling House of Zhao)." Sima Qian, 1806.
[206] The first large-scale government market system between the Xiongnu and Chinese was established by Han Wendi (r. 180-157 BCE), although private trade between the two parties had probably existed on the border for some time. Yü Ying-shih, "Han Foreign Relations," In *The Cambridge History of China, Vol. I: The Ch'in and Han Empires, 221 B.C.—A.D. 220*, edited by Denis Twitchett and Michael Loewe (Cambridge: Cambridge University Press, 1986), 388.

The furs of sables, marmots, foxes and badgers, colored rugs and decorated
carpets fill the Imperial Treasury… foreign products keep flowing in…[207]

Within this context, the figure of the mounted archer was added to the iconographic

vocabulary of the hunt in ancient China. Its popularity was due to a pervasive interest in foreign

goods during the Western Han, Xiongnu military might and firsthand encounters with the

Xiongnu in full regalia on diplomatic missions to the Western Han capital of Chang'an.[208] This

web of associations insured that it remained a popular motif decorating tomb goods throughout

the Western Han dynasty.

Although the figure of the mounted archer continued to decorate hill jars during the

Eastern Han, by the beginning of the first century CE, the popularity of this imagery had begun

to wane. This was due to the decline of the power of the court to dictate taste, the reemergence of

regional art traditions, and the costly and often unsuccessful wars waged against the Xiongnu. It

is likely that such factors led to the decline of the presence of the mounted archer in hunting

imagery and the development of the regional hunting iconography outlined in 3.0.

It is notable that that the mounted archer reappears in hunting scenes in tombs in Shaanxi

towards the end of the first century CE. As I will show, the return of the mounted archer in this

region was not simply due to the geographical closeness of this area to the old Western Han

capital, the work of provincial artists who were behind the times in tomb decoration, or a

reflection of the mixed economy and culture of the region. Instead, as I argue below, the

popularity of the mounted archer was due to the tradition of the hunt as a form of military

---

[207] Huan Kuan, *Yan tie lun* (Shanghai: Shanghai remnin chubanshe, 1974), 5. Translation see
Esson M. Gale, trans., *Discourses on Salt and Iron* (Leyden: E.J. Brill, Ltd., 1931), 14-15.
[208] Esther Jacobson, "Mountains and Nomads: A Reconsideration of the Origins of Chinese
Landscape Representation," 144-145.

training in ancient China and the idea of the mounted archer as the ultimate warrior who could defeat the Xiongnu.


## 5.2    FALCONRY


Although the mounted archer is the most conspicuous motif in the Northwest to be connected to the Xiongnu, scenes of falconry in these tombs also depict an activity that was probably associated with Northern nomadic peoples. Like the images of mounted archers in the region, the five reliefs that directly attest to the use of birds of prey in the hunt follow a set iconographic formula. In reliefs excavated from Suide, Mizhi and Yulin, Shaanxi, and Lishi, Shanxi, birds perch on the wrists of mounted riders.[209] Several reliefs from Dabaodang, Shenmu, Shaanxi (Tomb M1 and M23), may also illustrate scenes of falconry and show a bird of prey grasping another animal in its claws.[210] A raptor that has brought a small animal to the ground in front of a mounted falconer on a relief from Mizhi, supports this identification.[211]

Our understanding of the significance of falconry scenes in Shaanxi and Shanxi is complicated by the absence of visual, textual and archaeological materials that attest to the practice of falconry in ancient China. Based on visual and textual sources, the use of birds of prey in the hunt appears to have begun during the Han dynasty.[212] Texts record the use of hawks

---

[209] *Zhongguo huaxiangshi quanji*, Vol. 5, Fig. 35.
[210] Shaanxi sheng kaogu yanjiusui and Yulin shi wenwu guanli weiyuan hui, Fig. 37.
[211] *Zhongguo huaxiangshi quanji*, Vol. 5, Fig. 35.
Shaanxi sheng kaogu yanjiusuo 陝西省考古研究所 and Yulin shi wenwu guanli weiyuan hui [212] Possible earlier references to the practice of falconry are based on apocryphal texts or those which no longer exist. A medieval story argues for the practice of falconry in China as early as the Spring and Autumn period (770-475 BCE) and records that Chu Wen Wang (689-677 BCE)

and hounds by hunting enthusiasts, including Empress Deng (81-121 CE). Apart from a passage

from the *Xijing zaji* (*Miscellanies of the Western Capital*), that provides accurate descriptions of

goshawks and sparrow hawks, most textual records offer little insight into the practice of

falconry at this time.[213] Other texts suggest that during the Eastern Han dynasty falconry was

considered a pursuit of the wealthy and deemed frivolous, like horseracing, cockfighting and

hunting with hounds.

Eastern Han depictions of falconry provide the best evidence for practice of hunting with

raptors. A few scattered scenes of falconry are illustrated on tomb bricks and reliefs from

Shandong, Jiangsu and Sichuan and depict birds perched atop the wrist of a falconer who is on

---

hunted with a goshawk at Yunmeng. A Song dynasty encyclopedia, quoting the *Shi ji*, says that
when the prime minister of Qin, Li Si (c.280-208 BCE), was about to be executed he reminisced
about hunting with, "a yellow dog and a gray hawk on his arm." The reference to the gray hawk
in this passage however does not appear in modern editions of the *Shi ji*. This story seems to
have been prevalent as early as the Tang dynasty (618-906 CE) and is referenced in the
anonymous Tang poem, "Rhapsody on a Gray Goshawk." See Edward H. Schafer, "Falconry in
T'ang Times," *T'oung Pao* 46 (1958), 294-295. In William Charles White's book of tomb tiles
from the Luoyang area he identifies several images of birds as attesting to the practice of
falconry in ancient China. As noted by J.J.L. Duyvendak the third century BCE date he attributes
to these tiles is too early. The images themselves also simply depict flying birds and do not offer
strong support for the existence of falconry in ancient China. William Charles White, *Tomb Tile
Pictures of Ancient China; an Archaeological Study of Pottery Tiles from the Tombs of Western
Honan, dating about the Third Century BCE* (Toronto: The University of Toronto Press, 1939),
59, Plates 28, 108, 109. For J.J.L. Duyvendak's review of White's work see *T'oung Pao*, Second
Series, Vol. 35, No. 5 (1940), 371-376.
[213] Zhang Heng, "Xijing fu (Western Capital Rhapsody)," lines 555-560, possibly also line 460.
Translation see David R. Knechtges, trans., *Wen Xuan, or, Selections of Refined Literature*, 1:
221. Falconry in the Western Capital Rhapsody is noted by Duyvendak, 373; *Dongguan Han ji*:
"Hexi Deng huanghou (Empress Hexi Deng)." Wu Shuping, *Dongguan Han ji jiaozhu*, Vol. 1
(Zhengzhou: Zhongzhou guji chubanshe: Henan sheng xinhua shudian faxing, 1987), 205; *Hou
Han Shu* 64, "Liang Ji zhuan (Biography of Liang Ji)" and 105, "Yuan Shu zhuan (Biography of
Yuan Shu)." Fan Ye, 829, 1485; *Xijng zaji*: "Ying quan qi ming." Ge Hong, *Xijing zaji* (Xi'an:
San Qin chubanshe, 2006), 202. Cited in Schafer, 296, fn. 2.

foot and accompanied by hounds.[214] The iconographic differences between scenes of falconry

from the Northwest and those from Shandong, Sichuan and Jiangsu are probably the result of

different regional topographies. Falconry on foot would have been better suited to the wooded

areas of Shandong, Jiangsu and Sichuan, whereas, historically, falconry on horseback has been

practiced in continuous, open landscapes such as the plains/deserts of northern Shaanxi and

Shanxi. Under such conditions, the flight of both the predator and prey occurs over greater

distances than in wooded areas and necessitates the use of horses. The falconer could carry his

hawk through the field, cast her off when suitable prey had been found, follow her and dismount

to retrieve the bird after a kill.[215] The use of hunting hounds or horses in long-distance falconry

in Eastern Han China, were not mutually exclusive, as can be seen in several reliefs from the

Northwest.[216]

It is generally thought that the practice of falconry entered China via the west or the

north.[217] Several artifacts excavated from tombs associated with the Xiongnu suggest that the use

of birds of prey in the hunt was first learned by the Chinese from their northern neighbors. The

strongest evidence for the practice of falconry among the Xiongnu can be found on a second

century BCE bronze plaque excavated at Xichagou, Liaoning that depicts two riders on fantastic

---

[214] *Zhongguo huaxiangshi quanji*, Vol. 1, Fig. 95. I have not been able to find the tomb brick
from Sichuan that is described by Wen Qing in "Guanghan suo chu yongyuan ba nian zhuanba—
guanyu gudai yinglie de yize zhaji (An Inscription on a Tomb Brick Dating to 96 CE Excavated
from Guanghan—A Note Concerning Ancient Falconry), *Sichuan daxue xuebao* (*zhexue shehui
kexue ban*) 1985(02), 61-62.
[215] Adrian Walker, *The Encyclopedia of Falconry* (Lanham, MD and New York: The Derrydale
Press, 1999), 72-73.
[216] Li Lin, Kang Lanying and Zhao Liguang, 226-227, Fig. 664 and *Zhongguo huaxiangshi
quanji*, Vol. 1, Fig. 95.
[217] Edward Schafer, "Falconry in T'ang Times," 293.

animals with raptor-headed appendages. One figure carries a bird of prey on his right wrist.[218] A later belt plaque, dated to the second or first century BCE depicts a bird of prey seated on the rump of an equid pulling a cart followed by a hunting hound.[219] The frequency with which mounted falconers are depicted in the Northwest also suggests a familiarity with the practice of falconry by the Han Chinese who lived in this region and were in close proximity to experienced falconers.


### 5.3    HUMAN-ANIMAL COMBAT


The final subject in tomb reliefs from the Northwest that can be associated with foreigners and probably the Xiongnu are scenes of human-animal combat. These scenes, like their earlier counterparts in Nanyang, Henan, decorate door lintels in Shaanxi. Scenes of human-animal combat in this region draw on earlier reliefs from Nanyang, but exhibit a number of regional variations. Like other hunting imagery in the Northwest, they are fairly repetitive and focus on several human combatants who battle tigers, bears or fantastic animals. These include figures with swords and shields, lances, bows and arrows and mounted archers.[220] These figures, like their counterparts in reliefs from Nanyang, are depicted as foreigners. They have exaggerated facial features and wear strange headgear and clothing. Unlike the figures from Nanyang, none of these combatants are bare-chested and they wear long pants instead of billowy

---

[218] Tian Guangjin and Guo Suxin, *E'erduosi shi qing tong qi* (*Ordos Bronzes*) (Beijing: Wenwu chubanshe: Xinhua shudian Beijing faxing suo faxing, 1986) 73, Fig. 39.2.

[219] Emma C. Bunker with Trudy S. Kawami, Katheryn M. Linduff and Wu En, *Ancient Bronzes of the Eurasian Steppes from the Arthur M. Sackler Collections* (New York: Arthur M. Sackler Foundation, distributed by Abrams, 1997), 80, 273-276, No. 243.

[220] Li Guilong and Wang Jianqin, Fig. 13.

shorts and don different headgear. These figures can also be contrasted with many of the individuals that are represented as mounted archers or falconers in Shaanxi and Shanxi that are typically depicted as Han Chinese.[221] As previously stated, scenes of human-animal combat are related to hunting imagery on Warring States pictorial bronzes and the jiaodi xi (competitive games). Visual and textual evidence suggests that during the Han dynasty such imagery and the jiaodi xi were associated with the Xiongnu.

Images of human-animal combat first appear on Warring States pictorial bronzes. Stylistically, the representation of many of the real and imaginary creatures on these vessels appear to have been adopted and adapted from the art of the Northern Steppes, departing from the traditional stylized representation of animals on Shang and Western Zhou bronzes.[222] This imagery undoubtedly served as a precursor to Han depictions of human-animal combat and

---

[221] Although these differences suggest that the figures in scenes of human-animal combat from Shaanxi may represent the Xiongnu, foreigners are stereotypically portrayed in Han textual and visual sources making direct equations between pictorial representations and actual peoples difficult. See Xing Yitian, "Gudai Zhongguo ji Ou Ya wenxian tuxiang yu kaogu ziliao zhong de 'hu ren' waimao (The Appearance of 'Barbarians' as Seen in Ancient Chinese and Non-Chinese Literary, Pictorial and Archaeological Sources)," *Meishu shi yanjiu jikan* 9 (2000), 15-99.

[222] Alain Thote, "Some Remarks on Early Inlaid Pictorial Bronzes," *Orientations* 29, No. 10 (November 1998), 63; Charles D. Weber, *Chinese Pictorial Decoration of the Late Chou Period* (Ascona, Switzerland: Artibus Asiae Publishers, 1968), 137. As Thote notes, however, the adoption of a naturalistic form of representation does not account for the narrative form of representation found on these vessels. For an opposing view see Esther Jacobson, "Beyond the Frontier: A Reconsideration of Cultural Interchange between China and the Early Nomads," 223-227. Jacobson argues that the Chinese would have been familiar with a wide array of nomadic material culture and that capes, headdresses, saddles, bridles and other weapons were illustrated with individual images that together explained larger narrative structures. As Weber was the first to note in regards to inlaid bronzes, elements adopted from the art of the steppe were quickly adapted by the Chinese. Charles D. Weber, 236-237. For a more detailed analysis of motifs that may have been borrowed from nomadic sources and the debates regarding the nature and extent of such borrowing see Emma Bunker, "Sources of Foreign Elements in the Culture of the Eastern Zhou," In *The Great Bronze Age of China: A Symposium*, edited by George Kuwayama (Los Angeles: Los Angeles County Museum of Art, 1983), 84-93 and Esther Jacobson, "Beyond the Frontier: A Reconsideration of Cultural Interchange between China and the Early Nomads."

suggests that from an early time this motif may have been associated with northern nomadic peoples.

Although the peoples living to the north of China during the early Warring States period were not yet incorporated in the Xiongnu system, visual and textual evidence suggests that during the Han dynasty wrestling and combat between men and animals was connected in the Han mind with their northern enemy. The actual performance of such competitions in northern nomadic culture is suggested by a pair of second century BCE openwork bronze belt plaques excavated from the burial of a Xiongnu official near the Han capital of Chang'an (Kexingzhuang Tomb No. 140).[223] On these plaques, two figures are depicted wrestling. The owner of this plaque may have been part of a Xiongnu raiding party that came very close to the Han capital in 166 BCE. These depictions seem to be part of a more extensive Eurasian pictorial tradition of narrative scenes that probably decorated woven clothes and appliqué murals.[224]

Connections between the Xiongnu, wrestling and human-animal combat are further supported by the performances of the jiaodi xi staged by emperors for Xiongnu dignitaries during the Han dynasty that included a number of competitions as well as dramatic performances.[225] These performances suggest that to the Han elite, competitions between individuals and animals were considered an appropriate form of entertainment that would impress the Xiongnu visiting the capital. This assumption was probably strengthened by the Han belief that the Xiongnu and

---

[223] Jessica Rawson and Emma C. Bunker, *Ancient Chinese and Ordos Bronzes* (Hong Kong: The Oriental Ceramic Society of Hong Kong, 1990), Fig. 221.

[224] Emma C. Bunker with Trudy S. Kawami, Katheryn M. Linduff and Wu En, 85-86; Jessica Rawson and Emma C. Bunker, *Ancient Chinese and Ordos Bronzes* (Hong Kong: Oriental Ceramics Society of Hong Kong, 1990), No. 221.

[225] See Dubs and Loewe for an outline of the historical sources which document the circumstances under which the jiaodi xi were performed. Ban Gu, *History of the Former Han Dynasty*, translated by Homer H. Dubs, 2:129-131; Michael Loewe, *Divination, Mythology and Monarchy in Han China*, 236-237.

foreigners in general, had animal-like characteristics (see below). These beliefs may have meant that the Xiongnu were believed to be more capable of fighting tigers, bears and other ferocious beasts because of their animal-like nature.[226]

## 5.4    THE HUNT, WARFARE AND MILITARY TRAINING

Although the popularity of mounted archers, mounted falconers and human-animal combat in hunting scenes from the Northwest was connected to aspects of Xiongnu life, hunting imagery was also strongly associated in this region with the use of the hunt as a form of military training and displays of martial prowess in ancient China. Hunting may have been equated with warfare as early as the Shang dynasty (c. 1500-1050 BCE), but by the late Spring and Autumn period (770-475 BCE), hunting and warfare were inseparably linked in both linguistic usage and law. For example, the *Zuo Zhuan* (*The Commentary of Zuo*), records that as early as the seventh century BCE, the Grand Tutor of Jin was responsible for choosing the sites of hunts to be used in military training and the commanders for the state's armies. Whoever was given charge of the spring hunt in the following year also become commander-in-chief of the army. Other Eastern Zhou (770-256 BCE) texts record connections between hunting and warfare and in the *Shi jing* (*Book of Songs*), hunting and military prowess are eulogized in terms that are one in the same.[227]

This relationship between hunting and warfare continued during the Qin and Han dynasties. For example, in the "Liyi zhi (Treatise on Ritual)" in the *Hou Han shu*, military

---

[226] Roel Sterckx, *The Animal and the Daemon in Early China*, 108, 159-161.
[227] Mark Edward Lewis, *Sanctioned Violence in Early China*, 18, 35; *Zuo zhuan*, Lord Wen, year 6, 544-545, 552-553.

exercises are recorded as part of the Quliu, a festival held during the autumn when the emperor hunted game to be offered to the ancestors at imperial tombs. At this time, the *Hou Han shu* records,

> 遣使者齎束帛以賜武官。武官肄兵，習戰陣之儀、斬牲之禮，名曰貙劉。兵, 官皆肄孫、吳兵法六十四陣，名曰乘之.

> Messengers are sent to give bundles of silk as presents to military officers, who drill the troops in military formations. The ceremony of slaughtering the sacrificial victims is known as the Ch'u-liu. The drilling by the troops in the sixty-four formations of the art of Sun and Wu is known as the *shengchi*.[228]

The timing and performance of these activities during the Quliu festival seems to have followed seasonal associations advocated in several passages from the "Yue ling (Monthly Ordinances)" of the *Lüshi chunqiu* (*Mr. Lü's Spring and Autumn Annals*). This third century BCE compilation regulates hunting and military training to the declining months of the year that were viewed as a as a natural time of cold, death and decay.[229]

In the *Zhou li* (*Rites of Zhou*), hunting is also part of the "*Da yue* (Grand Review)," an elaborate military assessment which occurs in the eleventh month. This text seems to have provided the basis for the Grand Review described in Zhang Heng's (78-139 CE) *Dongjing fu* (*Eastern Capital Rhapsody*), a review held in the Western Park in the eleventh month. This review included complex military maneuvers and hunting. The possibility that smaller, but similar military inspections/exercises occurred in the commanderies during the Han dynasty is supported by several inscriptions on wooden strips excavated from Juyan (Edsen gol), Gansu, a military settlement during the Han dynasty. These inscriptions do not specifically mention

---

[228] Translation see Derk Bodde, 328. *Hou Han shu* 15, "Liyi zhi (Treatise on Ritual)." Fan Ye, 3122.

[229] Derk Bodde, 330. These particular passages are found in the 9th and 10th months. Chen Qiyou, *Lüshi chunqiu xin jiaoshi*, 474, 523. Translation see Knoblock and Riegel, 208, 225-226.

hunting, but they record archery competitions held during the autumn, a season that was traditionally associated with hunting and the military.[230]

It is not certain if reviews took place in Shang and Xihe commanderies of the Northwest, but hunting imagery from this region is strongly grounded in the tradition that associated hunting with military reviews and martial prowess. As noted in the Chapter 1, some of the occupants of these tombs served as officers in the Han army. The civilians who commissioned these tombs probably also had connections with both the Han military apparatus along the Northern Frontier and/or Xiongnu warriors. As soldiers and civilians living in militarized settlements, it is likely that the hunt was not practiced for subsistence, but for military training and recreation as well.

It is possible that a whole complex of recreational hunting intertwined with military training related to the subjugation of colonized peoples and the exploitation of natural resources lay behind the scenes of the hunt that decorate these tombs. Sadly our resources are too limited to explore such a possibility and its implications for hunting imagery in the Northwest. But, as several scholars have noted, the relationship between these reliefs and the military training of the patrons of these images is beyond doubt. The significance of such imagery in tombs is not simply an uncomplicated reflection of the exploits of the deceased as these scholars have suggested.[231] Instead in what follows, I will argue that in Shaanxi and Shanxi hunting imagery and its traditional relationship with warfare and military training helped to define a regional conception of the afterlife that was based on the relationship between the patrons of these images and their foreign neighbors.

---

[230] In the *Zhou li* hunting and military exercises are not confined to the seasons of autumn and winter, but also take place in the middle month of each season. Derk Bodde, 330, 351, 356-357. *Zhou li* 29/4a-9b; 29/6b-9b. Translation see David R. Knechtges, 1: 287-291.

[231] See Chapter 2 (3.0) for a general review of this scholarship.

This complicated relationship and its effect on the conception of the afterlife in the Northwest was based upon general Han beliefs that the Xiongnu were animal-like barbarians who lived in a barren wasteland. Although falconry and scenes of human-animal combat were connected in the Han mind to the lifestyle of northern nomadic pastoralists, during the Han dynasty, the figure of the mounted archer became the defining image of the Xiongnu in Han textual sources. Before examining texts that describe the Xiongnu as bestial and their homeland as inhospitable, I will argue that the popularity of the mounted archer in this region was based on the idea of the Xiongnu as the mounted archer extraordinaire. I suggest that imagery from the Northwest was dependent upon changes in the concept of the ideal warrior during the Western Han. These changes were the result of developments in the Han army and military tactics brought about by the initial superiority of the mobile Xiongnu cavalry.

Although a fascination with many aspects of Xiongnu culture is attested in visual and textual sources during the Western Han, the Xiongnu were viewed in this period as hostile barbarians who threatened the Chinese way of life. The introduction to *Shi ji* 110, "Xiongnu liezhuan (Account of the Xiongnu)," summaries the many ways in which the Xiongnu were considered to be different from the Chinese:

> 逐水草遷徙，毋城郭常處耕田之業，然亦各有分地. 毋文書，以言語為約束.
> 兒能騎羊，引弓射鳥鼠；少長則射狐兔：用為食. 士力能毋弓，盡為甲騎. 其
> 俗，寬則隨畜，因射獵禽獸為生業，急則人習戰攻以侵伐，其天性也.

> They move about in search of water and pasture and have no walled cities or fixed dwellings, nor do they engage in any kind of agriculture. They have no writing, and even promises and agreements are only verbal. The little boys start out by learning to ride sheep and shoot birds with a bow and arrow, and when they get a

little older they shoot foxes and hares, which are used for food. Thus all young men are able to use a bow and act as armed cavalry in time of war. It is their custom to herd their flocks in times of peace and make their living by hunting, but in times of crisis they go off on plundering and marauding expeditions. This seems to be their inborn nature.[232]

Throughout the *Shi ji* and other Han sources, the Xiongnu are frequently presented as an antithetical "other" living a semi-nomadic lifestyle, not having writing, not honoring the aged, etc. All of these differences, moreover, are usually summarized in their epithet as "the people who live by drawing the bow" in contast to the Han who "wear caps and girdles."

I suggest that the initial popularity of the motif of the mounted archer during the Western Han dynasty was prompted by these associations and was inspired by the success of the Xiongnu in building an empire that threatened and rivaled the Han. Although the use of mounted cavalry had been introduced in the Chinese army during the Warring States period, the Qin and early Han armies were mainly composed of foot soldiers. The first, ill-fated campaign against the Xiongnu in 201 BCE proved the superiority of the Xiongnu mounted warriors over the Chinese infantry. Economic instability during the early years of the Han dynasty prevented large-scale horse breeding and the expansion of the Han cavalry. But by the reign of Jingdi (156-141 BCE), thirty-six grazing grounds where horses were broken and trained were created in the north and west to combat the superiority of the Xiongnu mounted cavalry.[233]

By the end of the second century BCE, the use of the chariot in battle, so frequently eulogized in the *Shi jing*, had given way to an army comprised of mounted cavalry. Although

---

[232] *Shi ji* 110, "Xiongnu liezhuan (Account of the Xionngu)." Sima Qian, 2879. Translation see Sima Qian, *Records of the Grand Historian: Han Dynasty*, II, 129.
[233] Michèle Pirazzoli-t'Serstevens, *The Han Dynasty*, translated by Janet Seligman (New York: Rizzoli, 1982), 30, 90. Also see Chang Chun-shu for a discussion of Han Wudi's campaigns agains the Xiongnu and the importance of horses and mounted cavalry. Chang Chun-shu, "Military Aspect of Han Wu-ti's Campaigns," *Harvard Journal of Asiatic Studies* 26 (1966), 148-173.

this process had begun much earlier with the introduction of infantry and the development of massive armies through the extension of military service during the Eastern Zhou, it was the inability of the Han to deal with Xiongnu mounted warriors that signaled the abandonment of the war chariot in ancient China.[234] Han battle tactics were also adopted from the Xiongnu, with both sides engaging in maneuvers that consisted of small parties mostly made up of horseman. These parties raided enemy territory in order to displace the enemy, seize cattle and horses and provoke surrender.[235]

The threat of the Xiongnu and the adoption of new military tactics also meant that the model warrior of the Han dynasty could no longer be the generals and kings idealized in the *Shi jing* who are valorized through descriptions of their war chariots and their skillful movements across the field.[236] Instead we find that two of the most famous generals of the Western Han dynasty, Huo Qubing (140-117 BCE) and Li Guang (d. 119 BCE) are described in their biographies as skilled at riding and shooting. Although we are told in the *Shi ji*, that archery was passed down in Li's family for ages, the archery for which both he and Huo Qubing were known was not the kind practiced in the ritualized and anesthetized archery contests described in the *Shi jing, Zhou li* and *Li ji* (*Book of Rites*). Instead these generals are described as mobile riders who, through unconventional military tactics (ultimately derived from the Xiongnu), proved successful when other generals had failed. In Huo Qubing's first military foray, the *Shi ji* records that the general broke away from the main army with eight hundred men in search of grain and

---

[234] Mark Edward Lewis, *Sanctioned Violence in Early China*, 54-61.
[235] Michèle Pirazzoli-t'Serstevens, 90.
[236] For examples see Ode No. 198, "Xiao rong (Small War Chariot)," *Qin feng* (*Odes of* Qin) and No. 177, "Liu yüe (The Sixth Month)," *The Minor Odes*, "Tong Gong zhi shi (Decade of Tong Gong)." Translation see Waley, 100-101, 150-151.

killed or captured a large number of Xiongnu riders.[237] It was tactics like these, along with their skill as mounted archers, that caused these generals to be respected and feared by the both the Han and the Xiongnu.

By the time the figure of the mounted archer reappears in the tombs from the Northwest in the first century CE, the power of the Xiongnu and the type of generals and army that could defeat them must have been firmly entrenched in the Han mind. Due to the proximity of their mounted enemy, military training in Shang and Xihe commanderies must have focused on developing the same skills that had made Huo Qubing and Li Guang famous. Thus the mounted archers in these tombs were not associated only with the foreign lifestyles of the Xiongnu, but were also seen as the means to engage and defeat the enemy.

## 5.6    XIONGNU LANDS AS THE ENDS OF THE EARTH/WILDERNESS

In this region, Han associations of the mounted archer with the Xiongnu were expanded in a regional conception of the afterlife that blended elements of Han mortuary belief with positive and negative conceptions of the Xionngu. I suggest that the mounted archers in tombs from the Northwest were dispatched to combat the dangers that confronted the deceased on their journey to paradise. The conflation of the perilous borderlands between Heaven and Earth with the world of the Xiongnu is corroborated by Han texts that describe the Xiongnu lands as a

---

[237] *Shi ji* 109, "Li Guang liezhuan (Biography of Li Guang)" and *Shi ji* 111, "Wei Jiangjun Piaoqi liezhuan (Biography of General Wei Qing and the Swift Calvary General Huo Qubing)." Sima Qian, 2867-2878, 2928. Translation see Sima Qian, *Records of the Grand Historian: Han Dynasty*, 117-128; 169.

northern wilderness located at the ends of the earth. In the second poem from *Eighteen Songs on a Normad Flute*, Cai Wenji (b.177) who was taken prisoner by the Xiongu in 195, laments,

> I was taken on horseback to the ends of the earth;
> Tiring of life, I sought death, but death would not come.
> The barbarians stink so. How can they be considered human?
> Their pleasures and angers are like the jackal and the wolf-how unbearable.
> We traveled to the end of the Tianshan, enduring all the frost and sleet;
> The customs are rude, the land is desolate-we are near the nomads' territories.
> An overcast sky stretches beyond ten thousand miles.  Not a single bird is in sight.
> The cold sands are boundless; one can no longer tell the south from the north.[238]

Although grounded in her own experience as a hostage in the North, Cai Wenji's description is based on stereotypes that are first expressed in "The Account of the Xiongnu (*Shi ji* 110)," where the Xiongnu domains are described as, "澤滷 swamps and saline wastes," a "匈奴处北地, 寒, 殺氣早降 land (where the) cold and the killing frosts come early," and "北寒苦無水草之地 north of the desert (where it is) cold and bitter (and) there is no water and pasture."[239]

Such bleak descriptions of the Xiongnu homeland resonate with Han and pre-Han conceptions of the afterlife. As we have seen in poems from the *Chu ci* (*Songs of the South*), Han dynasty tomb-quelling texts and a tomb inscription from Suide, Shaanxi, upon death it was believed that the deceased would find himself in a dangerous region between Heaven and Earth surrounded by ferocious animals, demons and monsters. The sacred geography of the *Shanhaijing* (*Classics of the Mountains and Seas*) supports these descriptions of the borderlands between Heaven and Earth describing countless oddities, uninhabitable lands and malignant spirits that travelers encounter as they move through the Middle Kingdom and the lands beyond.

---

[238] "Eighteen Songs of a Nomad Flute, Poem 2." Robert A. Rorex and Wen Fong, *Eighteen Songs of a Nomad Flute; the Story of Lady Wen-chi: A Fourteenth-century Handscroll in the Metropolitan Museum of Art* (New York: Metropolitan Museum of Art; distributed by New York Graphic Society Greenwich, Connecticut, 1974).

[239] *Shi ji* 110, "The Account of the Xiongnu." Sima Qian, 2896, 2903, 2912. Translation see Sima Qian, *Records of the Grand Historian: Han Dynasty* II, 141, 146, 155.

Based on these texts, I suggest that in tombs from the Northwest, the mounted archer and other motifs associated with Xiongnu life suggest a parallel between the barren wastelands of the beyond and what was believed to be the desolate topography of the Xiongnu domain. The fact that the Han believed the Xionngu lived in a territory very close to the ends of the earth is supported by comments made by Wang Chong (27- c.100 CE) in the *Lunheng* (*Critical Essays*), who remarked, "匈奴之北，地之邊陲 The north of the Xiongnu is the border-land of the earth."[240] That the domains of the Xiongnu became associated with the wilderness of the afterlife may also be supported by the traditional Chinese belief that the North was the land of the dead.

These associaitons may have also been motivated by fear of being taken hostage to the Xiongnu lands, never to return. The story of the faithful official Su Wu (140-60 BCE) in the *Han shu* provides the quintessential account of the loyal Han official exiled in a barbarian land. During his nineteen-year-sojourn in the north, the *Han shu* records that Su Wu was forced to live on the desolate shores of Lake Baikal and eat the seeds of grass stored in the burrows of field mice.[241] The *Shi ji* and *Han shu* record that other less loyal officials surrendered, were rewarded by the Xiongnu leader and took up the Xiongnu life. We do not know the fate of many of the other soldiers and Chinese who settled this region and either surrendered to the Xiongnu in battle or were captured during raids. Although some may have fared well, those living in the Northwest must have had a constant fear of being captured during a Xiongnu uprising or raid and forced to live among the "barbarians" beyond the Great Wall.

---

[240] Wang Chong, *Lunheng* 11.2, "Shuo ri (Speaking of the Sun)." Wang Chong, 171. Translation see Alfred Forke, 263.

[241] *Han Shu* 54, "Li Guang Su Jian zhuan (The Biographies of Li Guang and Su Jian)." Ban Gu, 2450-2470. Translation see Burton Watson, *Courtier and Commoner in Ancient China, Selections from the History of the Former Han by Pan Ku* (New York and London: Columbia University Press, 1974), 34-45.

I suggest that these fears had a direct impact on the conception of the afterlife in tombs in Shaanxi and Shanxi. In hunting imagery from this region the fears of the patrons of these images of living (and dying) in exile in the inhospitable Xiongnu domains were subsumed into the horrors of the wilderness that confronted the deceased upon death. The coalescence of these two fears, was not due simply to the unwelcoming topography and climate of the Northern Steppe, but to Han ideas about the inhabitants of the region themselves.


**5.7     THE XIONGNU AS NON-HUMAN AND FOREIGNERS IN HAN TOMBS**


Visual representations of foreigners during the Han dynasty provide another point of comparison that supports a connection between the Northern Steppe and the borderlands that awaited the deceased upon death. These depictions, corroborated by textual descriptions of the Xionngu and other foreigners as animals or animal-like, suggest that the northern nomads could have joined the denizens of the afterlife in tombs from this region. Although there are not many depictions of foreigners in the Northwest apart from the figures represented in scenes of human-animal combat, the few representations that survive can, with the help of other Han visual and textual records, be used to establish the multivalent purposes of and complicated attitudes toward foreigners in the Northwest.

Based on Han and pre-Han visual and textual records, the fantastic creatures that inhabited the regions between Heaven and Earth were conceived as animal-animal and man-animal hybrids. In the Northwest, immortals (*xian*) are often depicted in reliefs as avian hybrids, their hybrid form suggesting the power of metamorphosis and ability to travel to and from paradise. Immortals were one of the few beings that occupied the realms between Heaven and

Earth that were believed to be benign creatures; most of these inhabitants are depicted as evil and capricious spirits that seek to harm the deceased or the traveler at any turn. I suggest that the Xiongnu, like other foreigners, through their virtue of living geographically and culturally on the periphery of Chinese civilization were considered part of this other world. Whether they were perceived as benevolent or malignant creatures in the Northwest is complicated by Han conceptions of foreigners in general, because the marginality of foreigners could be seen as both a positive and negative attribute.

In Eastern Han dynasty tomb reliefs, foreigners are often depicted as man-animal hybrids and/or represented alongside immortals and other auspicious creatures. In a relief from Linyi, Shandong, a foreigner is shown with a pair of immortals and has a pointed cap, exaggerated nose and facial hair. The lower half of his body, subsumed in swirling clouds is more merman-like than human.[242] Similar figures with pointed caps, scales or fine hair are depicted on the stone columns of the front chamber at Yi'nan, Shandong.[243] These figures suggest that foreigners, like immortals were often seen as being half-man and half-animal. Since foreigners occupied the fringe of the Chinese world, they like immortals were viewed as spiritually empowered figures that could assist the deceased in his journey to paradise.[244]

Similar associations inform the representation of three figures that appear in a hunting scene depicted on a door lintel excavated at Dangjiagou, Mizhi, Shaanxi, that shows two mounted archers and another archer on foot.[245] The mounted archer on the left has a bear-like

---

[242] Zheng Yan, "Barbarian Images in Han Period Art," *Orientations*, Vol. 29, No. 6 (June 1998), Fig. 3.

[243] *Zhongguo huaxiang shi quanji*, Vol. 1, Fig. 202.

[244] Zheng Yan, "Barbarian Images in Han Period Art," *Orientations*, Vol. 29, No. 6 (June 1998), 50-53.

[245] Li Lin, Kang Lanying and Zhao Liguang, Fig. 25.

face and his companion on the right has rounded animal-like ears atop his head. The third figure appears human, but with his long tunic, baggy pants, broad face and strange hair/headdress, he may represent a Xiongnu warrio. His clothing/headgear is unlike the other hunters in the region and has more in common with the foreigners depicted in scenes of human-animal combat. That the figures in the hunting scene from Dangjiagou represented the Xiongnu, or at the very least foreigners, is also supported by the fact that the tunic worn by the bear-headed figure buttons on the left side, a recurring characteristic of foreigners in Han texts.[246]

The physical characteristics and dress of these figures, together with the dragon ridden by the figure on the right, underscores the otherworldly nature of this scene. I suggest that these three figures represent foreigners, possibly Xionngu, who like the Chinese archers in the region, are represented battling the demons and dangerous animals that attempt to block the soul of the deceased during its journey. This interpretation and the success of their endeavor is indicated by the two winged figures in the central pavilion that probably represent the deceased.[247]

This relief together with those depicting foreigners, engaged in human-animal combat imply that in the Northwest, foreigners, because of their marginality and their close ties to the animal world were believed to be appropriate figures to battle the malignant spirit that inhabited the borderlands between Heaven and Earth. Such powers were based on the general belief that

---

[246] For a survey of the ways in which foreigners are depicted in Han dynasty visual and textual sources, the differences between the two records and the difficulty of equating any figures with specific foreign peoples see Xing Yitian, "Gudai Zhongguo ji Ou Ya wenxian tuxiang yu kaogu ziliao zhong de 'hu ren' waimao (The Appearance of 'Barbarians' as Seen in Ancient Chinese and Non-Chinese Literary, Pictorial and Archaeological Sources)."

[247] These figures could also represent Xiwangmu and Dongwanggong; however the goddess and god are also represented (in their chicken and cow-headed forms) on the stones that flank either side of the tomb door.

foreigners, because they were in closer contact with or were part of the animal world, were expert hunters, animal tamers and herders.[248]

The idea that foreigners were closer to or actually animals had a much darker side in Han texts. With regards to the Xiongnu, this view is expressed by Han Anguo (d. 127 BCE) in the *Shi ji*:

今匈奴負戎馬之足，懷禽獸之心，遷徙鳥舉，難得而制也. 得其地不足以為廣，有其眾不足以為彊，自上古不屬為人.

The Xiongnu move on the feet of swift war horses, and in their breasts beat the hearts of beasts. They shift from place to place as fast as a flock of birds, so that it is difficult to corner them and bring them under control. Though we win possession of their land, it would be no great addition to the empire, and though we ruled their hosts of warriors, they would do little to strengthen our power. From the most ancient times the Xiongnu have never been regarded as a part of humanity.[249]

This along with other passages show that the Han Chinese considered the Xiongnu to be part of the animal rather than the human world and to be both an aberration and a threat to the existing order. These attributes would have made them fitting companions to the ferocious hybrid creatures that inhabited the borderlands of the afterlife.

The possibility that the Xiongnu could have joined these less felicitous creatures in the Northwest is supported by Han reliefs depicting scenes of battle between Barbarian and Han forces (*Hu Han jiaozheng tu/Hu Han zhanzheng tu*). Some of these reliefs, such as the stone over the entrance to the tomb at Yi'nan depict a battle between Barbarian and Han forces that takes place on a bridge.[250] The battle illustrated on the west wall of the Xiaotangshan shrine shows a more typical representation of this imagery and depicts a host of Barbarians emerging from

---

[248] Roel Sterckx, *The Animal and the Daemon in Early China*, 108, 159-161.
[249] *Shi ji* 108, "Han Changru liezhuan (The Biography of Han Changru)." Sima Qian, 2861. Translation see Sima Qian, *Records of the Grand Historian: Han Dynasty* II, 112.
[250] *Zhongguo huaxiang shi quanji*, Vol. 1, Fig. 179.

mountains to engage Han forces.[251] It may be that the barbarians emerging from the mountains in these reliefs were meant to represent the Xionngu, as the major boundary and the site of many battles between Han and Xiongnu forces were the Yin Mountains in Inner Mongolia.[252]

Xin Lixiang, Lydia Thompson and Xing Yitian have argued that the barbarians depicted in some of these battle scenes represent forces that attempt to block the travels of the deceased. Xin has argued that Battle at the Bridge is symbolic of the battle between the forces of light and darkness and that the barbarians in these scenes are depicted as guardians of the netherworld. According to Xin, their defeat by Han warriors enabled the deceased to travel back and forth between the world of the dead and the ancestral shrine to receive sacrifices from his descendents. Lydia Thompson has argued that the barbarians illustrated in the Battle at the Bridge scene at Yi'nan represent demons that prevent the passage of the deceased to paradise and the Han soldiers in these scenes act as guardians and protectors of the dead. In a similar vein, Xing Yitian argues that some battle scenes between Barbarian and Han forces from Shandong show the deceased being escorted by gods to Mount Kunlun or Mount Tai. According to him, the barbarians in these scenes represent the obstacles that faced the deceased in their journey to the immortal world.[253]

Although not common in Shaanxi and Shanxi, a battle scene between Barbarian and Han forces decorates the west wall of the front chamber of a tomb excavated at Baijiashan, Suide,

---

[251] Ibid., Fig. 43.

[252] Xing Yitian, "Handai huaxiang Hu Han zhanzheng tu de goucheng, leixing yu yiyi (Composition, Types, and Significance of the Scene of Sino-Barbarian Battle in the Pictorial Art of Han China," *Meishu shi yanjiu jikan* 19 (2005), 90-91.

[253] Xin Lixiang, 328-334; Lydia Thompson, "The Yi'nan Tomb: Narrative and Ritual in Pictorial Art of the Eastern Han (25-220 C.E.)," (PhD Dissertation, New York University, 1998), 323-361. Cited in Zheng Yan, 59. Xing Yitian, "Handai huaxiang Hu Han zhanzheng tu de goucheng, leixing yu yiyi," 98.

Shaanxi.[254] In this relief, soldiers approach a hilly area surrounded by figures with drawn bows. In the foray, one figure has been decapitated, his headless body lies on the ground. This scene shares a number of elements with Sino-Barbarian Battle Scenes from Shandong and Jiangsu: its association with a hunting scene, the decapitated figure in the middle of the foray and the barbarians fleeing/coming from the mountains.

A major difference between this scene and other depictions of Sino-Barbarian Battles, however, is that the forces attacking the figures in the mountains wear two kinds of headgear and may represent different groups of people. This suggests to Xing Yitian that, since these figures include foreign soldiers, this scene should not be identified as a Sino-Barbarian Battle Scene. Although it is true that the Han forces wear both Han and non-Han costumes and headgear, the inclusion of the above listed elements that it shares with other Sino-Barbarian Battle Scenes suggests that it is a regional variant of this category. The rational for including troops wearing foreign headgear in this scene is offered by Xing when discussing a Captive Offering Scene that decorates a tomb relief also excavated from Suide, Shaanxi. This tomb relief also includes an ambiguous mixture of hairstyles and dress. Here he suggests that the unique headgear of some of these figures might have been worn by Han officials that had absorbed habits of their foreign neighbors while also noting that the soldiers who occupied posts along the frontier were often not Han Chinese.[255]

The same circumstances explain the ambiguity of the figures depicted in the battle scene from Suide. That the barbarian figures in this scene, like some of their counterparts in other regions, represented the obstacles that the deceased would face on his journey to paradise is

---

[254] Li Guilong and Wang Jianqin, Fig. 29.

[255] Xing Yitian, "Handai huaxiang Hu Han zhanzheng tu de goucheng, leixing yu yiyi," 70, 80-83.

suggested by other elements within the composition. To the right of the battle scene are humans and animals including several figures playing a game, two foreigners on a camel, grazing horses, other figures performing unidentifiable actions and a pair of humans and a pair of deer copulating. In general, the grazing animals, copulating figures and the foreigners may suggest fecundity and therefore rebirth.[256] On the other side of the battle is a hunting scene with animals fleeing through the mountains. A boar, deer, fox, birds and a dragon race toward the far left where several deer are depicted calmly eating the bark or leaves from trees.

Although some parts of this composition may have been randomly combined with others, a number of elements suggest that the barbarians depicted in the hills, like some figures in scenes from Shandong, represent demons or malignant spirits who are attempting to block the passage of the deceased. Foreigners in a hilly landscape, figures copulating, the dragon and the placid animals depicted on the far left create an atmosphere which suggests that the scenery and the actions taking place are not of this world. This interpretation is corroborated by the imagery depicted on the four vertical slabs that support this horizontal relief. These scenes depict immortals climbing on swirling tendrils that are an amalgamation of clouds and the fungus of immortality and two large towers whose climbing figures suggest an alternate route to paradise.

I argue that this scene at Suide, like hunting imagery in the Northwest and some battle scenes in other regions depicted and facilitated the passage of the deceased to paradise. The dangers that faced the deceased in this composition are represented by the foreigners lurking in the mountain who are being defeated by Han cavalry. The role of this imagery is further implied by elements in reliefs that depict scenes of the hunt and immortals frolicking with animals in this

---

[256] Images of foreigners were worshipped in some regions as fertility gods during the Han dynasty. Zheng Yan, 56.

region. These include the hunting scene itself and the docile animals on the far left of the composition that can be compared to the felicitous animals that frolic with immortals among mountainous clouds in other tombs. The figures copulating on the right are also similar to mating animals that appear among the cloudscapes frequented by immortals and animals in another relief from Suide.[257]

The representation of foreigners in hunting scenes and in this battle scene suggest a mixture of attitudes and feelings toward non-Han Chinese who could either thwart or aid the deceased on his journey to paradise, much as the living Xiongnu could either frustrate or help the Chinese living in the region.[258] Unfortunately it is difficult based on the representation of these figures to firmly identify them as Xiongnu by their physical characteristics and clothing/headgear due to the stereotyping of foreigners in Han visual culture. But it seems logical that such figures would have represented the foreigners with whom the patrons of these images had the most contact, regardless of the authenticity of their depiction.

---

[257] Copulating animals appear twice in the tomb of the Grand Administrator of Liaodong (Liaodong taishou), Huangjiata Tomb No. 7, Suide, Shaanxi. See Li Guilong and Wang Jianqin, Figs. 13 and 14.

[258] The few other representations of foreigners in this region support this interpretive dichotomy. A lintel from Shenmu depicts a foreign elephant-tamer and a mounted archer with a *tian ma* (heavenly horse) among a swirling cloudscape, see *Zhongguo huaxiang shi quanji* (*Collected Works of Chinese Tomb Reliefs*), Vol. 5, Fig. 223. A horizontal relief from Suide shows a procession with several foreigners traveling through the mountains and contains an embedded hunting scene (there is a mounted archer depicted in front of the mountain as in the scene that depicts the battle between Barbarian and Han forces); these foreigners were probably meant to protect the deceased on his journey. See Li Guilong and Wang Jianqin, Fig. 65. Similar foreign figures, one with a camel, are depicted in Lishi, Shanxi. See Li Lin, Kang Lanying and Zhao Liguang, Figs. 653 and 654. Similar imagery can also be seen on a relief from Yulin, Shaanxi; see *Zhongguo huaxiang shi quanji*, Vol. 5, Fig. 24. Another scene from Suide depicts a Barbarian king presented with gifts and prisoners of war, a scene that also appears in some Barbarian and Han battle scenes in Shandong and Jiangsu: Li Guilong and Wang Jianqin, Fig. 69. Another relief from Tomb No. 4, Mizhi, Shaanxi, depicts foreign warriors, but is damaged; see Li Lin, Kang Lanying and Zhao Liguang, Fig. 65.

The question that remains unanswered, however, is whether these foreigners were more frequently represented as auspicious or ominous figures among the borderlands between Heaven and Earth. The reliefs themselves do not strongly suggest either alternative and it may be that individual interpretations of such imagery varied. It appears that it was with a balanced mixture of appreciation and apprehension that non-Han Chinese were represented in tombs from the Northwest. This ambiguous relationship is visually realized in hunting imagery that depicts the Chinese as mounted archers, performing an activity adopted from the Xiongnu to combat their military power, in order to pass through the cold and barren regions of the afterlife. This imagery, as I have argued, suggests the complex nature of associations between the Xiongnu, their domains, northern nomadic life and representations of the afterlife in Shaanxi and Shanxi.


## 5.8    CONCLUSION


In this chapter I have examined the figure of the mounted archer and activities depicted in hunting scenes from the Northwest that were associated with the lifestyle of the Xiongnu. Rather than interpreting these scenes as reflections of the unique political and social environment of this region, I have argued that their depictions were based upon a vision of the afterlife that equated the world of the Xiongnu with the uninviting borderlands between Heaven and Earth. The fulcrum of such imagery was the figure of the mounted archer who through his adoption of Xiongnu military and hunting tactics was able to defeat the animals, malignant spirits and the Xiongnu themselves to insure the safe passage of the deceased to paradise.

The ambiguous nature of the mounted archer who assumes elements of the lifestyle of his enemies in order to defeat them is also present in the reliefs that depict foreigners in this region.

Sometimes, these figures are shown in hunting scenes where they are illustrated as aiding the soul of the deceased in its journey to paradise. In other scenes in Shaanxi and Shanxi, foreigners represent the malignant spirits that confronted the dead. Both sets of imagery, as well as the figure of the mounted archer expressed the complex nature of the relationship of Chinese settlers to their foreign neighbors who were conceived of as friend and foe to both the living and the dead. Such ambiguity was based on the mixed cultural and unstable political climate of the region that allowed the patron's fears of Xiongnu rebellion, possible exile and the Xiongnu themselves to be subsumed within their fears of the afterlife.

## 6.0    CONCLUSION


This dissertation has examined depictions of the hunt in Eastern Han tomb reliefs from Shaanxi and Shanxi arguing that they were placed in the tomb to represent and facilitate the passage of the deceased to the immortal paradise of Xiwangmu. My interpretation of this imagery has been informed by three overarching issues: 1) the idea that artifacts and images placed in Han tombs were not merely models but believed to become real guides, 2) the conception of the afterlife in ancient China as a journey and 3) the representations of and relationships between Han Chinese and "others" living inside and outside the borders of the Han Empire.

Fundamental to my study is the understanding of images of the hunt as active scenes that facilitated the passage of the soul of the deceased. More than mere reflections of the lifestyle of the deceased, I have argued that these images were placed in tombs because they were similar to the models of animals and other objects found in Han tombs that were understood as being both different from while at the same time equivalent to objects used by the living. As such, I have argued that these images were placed in tombs because it was believed that through their representation the passage of the deceased would become a reality; that is to say they did not simply depict the journey of the deceased, but were believed to literally become the journey of deceased. This is why hunters are often found flanking horse and chariot processions in reliefs throughout the region, protecting the spirit of the deceased from the dangerous spirits and beasts that haunted the borderlands between Heaven and Earth.

Although there is a growing body of materials which addresses the conception of the afterlife as a journey in Han and pre-Han China, my study has been the first to focus on the role of the hunt in this process. Based on visual and textual sources, I have argued that hunting was seen as having powerful exorcistic qualities and capable of establishing communication with Heaven through the meat it provided for ancestral sacrifices. Therefore in tomb reliefs from Shaanxi and Shanxi, scenes of the hunt were combined with images of immortals cavorting with animals because both sets of imagery cleared the path for the deceased and provided protection in the afterlife.

Finally, my interpretation of this imagery is also based on the understanding that those living in Shang and Xihe commanderies had meaningful relationships with peoples beyond the Han Empire, a fact that has been overlooked in previous scholarship. Since this imagery was greatly dependent upon the existence of this region as a Han colony and the non-Chinese living within and beyond its confines, the reliefs from this region have also served as a case study of cultural contact and the assimilation and the manipulation of certain elements of a foreign lifestyle within a mortuary context. I have suggested that these elements (mounted archer, human-animal combat scenes and scenes of falconry) were part of a larger set of regional mortuary traditions in Shang and Xihe commanderies that equated the borderlands between Heaven and Earth with the world of the Xiongnu.

My approach throughout has shown the necessity of discarding normative interpretations in the study of Eastern Han iconography. It has been based on the understanding that an analysis of imagery in Eastern Han tomb reliefs must include and be informed by the geographic, historical and cultural environment of the region in which they were made. The three themes outlined above do suggest that the hunt continued to play an important part in mortuary traditions during the Han dynasty. The power and function of scenes of the hunt in Shaanxi and Shanxi, however, can only be completely understood against the background of the turbulent and multicultural climate in which the patrons of these images lived.

# CHINESE GLOSSARY

Aidi 哀帝
Anding 安定
Anqiu 安丘
Anrenxiang 安仁鄉
Baihuatan 百花潭
*Baihutong* 白虎通
Baijiashan 百家山
*Baopuzi* 抱朴子
Bing 并
boshan lu 博山爐
Cai Wenji 蔡文姬
Cai Yong 蔡邕
Chen Pan 陳盤
Chengguanzhen 城關鎮
Chenliuzhuang 沈劉庄
Chi You 蚩尤
Chu 楚
*Chu ci* 楚辭
Chu Wen Wang 楚文王
Da nuo 大儺
Da yue 大閱
"Da Zhao" 大招
Dabaodang 大保當
Dangjiagou 黨家溝
Dayi 大邑
"Deng Chen liezhuan" 鄧寇列傳
"Deng she" 登涉
"Dili zhi xia" 地理誌下
Dongjiazhuang 董家庄
"Dongjing fu" 東京賦
Dongsheng 東胜
Dongwanggong 東王宮

*dou* 豆
*Du Liao jiangjun*□ 遼將軍
Duke of Shao 邵公
*duwei* 都尉
Empress Deng 鄧皇後
Fangcheng 方城
Fanchengyangji 方城楊集
*Fengsu tongyi* 風俗通義
Fengxiang 風翔
*fusang* 扶桑
Fugu 府谷
Fushi□ □
Fu Xi 伏羲
Gaowangsi 高王寺
Gaozhuang 高庄
Ge Hong 葛洪
Guanzhuang 官庄
"Gui Feng" 貴當
Han Anguo 韓安國
"Han Changru liezhuan" 韓長孺列傳
*Han shu* 漢書
Hejiagou 賀家溝
Hengshan 橫山
Hexi 河西
*hou* 候
*Hou Han shu* 後漢書
*hu* 壺

Hu Han jiaozheng tu/Hu Han zhanzheng tu 胡漢交戰圖/胡漢戰爭圖
*hu numen* 胡奴門

*Hu Qiang xiaowei* 護□□□

*Hu Wuhuan xiaowei* 護鳴□□□

*Huainanzi* 淮南子

Huangdi 黃帝

Huangjiata 黃家塔

Huashan 華山

Huo Qubing 霍去病

*jiaodi xi* 角抵戲

Jiaxiang 嘉祥

Jin 晉

Jingdi 景帝

Jinxi 晋西

"Jisi zhi" 祭祀誌

"Junguo zhi" 郡國誌

Junliugou 軍劉溝

Juyan 居延

La 腊

Li Guang 李廣

"Li Guang liezhuan" 李廣列傳

"Li Guang zhuan" 李廣軍傳

"Li Guang Su Jian zhuan" 李廣蘇建傳

Li Si 李斯

*Li ji* 禮記

Liang 梁

Liaodong taishou 遼東太守

*lie* 猎

*Liezi* 列子

Linyi 臨沂

*lingzhi* 靈芝

Lishi 离石

"Liu yüe" 六月

*Liubo* 六博

Liulige 琉璃阁

Liulin 柳林

Liyang 黎陽

"Liyi zhi" 禮儀志

"Lu ling" 鹿令

"Luan long" 亂龍

*Lunheng* 論衡

*Lunyu* 論語

Lü Simian 呂思勉

*Lüshi chunqiu* 呂氏春秋

Mamaozhuang 馬茂庄

Master Jining 济宁师

Mawangdui 馬王堆

Mingdi 明帝

Meiji 美稷

Meng Tian 蒙恬

"Meng Tian liezhuan" 蒙恬列傳

*Mingqi* 明器

Mizhi 米脂

Mount Kunlun 崑崙山

Mount Tai 泰山

*Nan Shanyu* 南單于

"Nan Xiongnu liezhuan" 南匈奴列傳

Niu Liping 牛李平

Nü Gua 女媧

Penglai 蓬莱

Pingding 平定

Pingshan 平山

"Pingzhun shu" 平準書

*po* 魄

*pushou* 鋪獸

*Qi Feng* 齊風

*Qianfu lun* 潛夫論

Qiang 羌

"Qin benji" 秦本紀

*Qin feng* 秦風

*qilin* 麒麟

Qingjian 清澗

*qionglong ding* 穹窿頂

*quan ding* 券頂

que 闕

Qiuci 龜茲

Qiuci guo 龜茲國

Quliu 貙劉

Sanpanshan 三盤山

*shan* 山

Shanbei 陝北

Shang (commandery) 上 (郡)

*Shanhaijing* 山海經

*Shao nan* 召南

*she hou* 射猴
*she que* 射雀
*shengchi* (sheng zhi) 乘之
Shenmu 神木
*Shi* 士
"Shi hun li" 士昏禮
*Shi ji* 史記
Shi jing 詩經
*Shi Xiongnu zhongliang jiang*
使匈奴中郎將
"Shuo ri" 說日
Shun 舜
*shizhe* 使者
Shoufeng 朔方
*shuguo* 屬國
Shundi 順帝
*Shuowen jiezi* 說文解字
*Si* 兕
"Si tie" 駟驖
Sishipu 四十鋪
Songshan 宋山
Su Wu 蘇武
Suide 綏德
*taishou* 太守
"Tang Wen" 湯問
*Taotie* 饕餮
Tian Fang 田魴
t'ien kuang (tian guang) 天光
*tian ma* 天馬
"Tong Gong zhi shi" 彤弓之什
*tun tian* 屯田
Wang Chong 王充
Wang Deyuan 王得元
Wang Fu 王符
Wang Junwei 王君威
"Wang Mang liezhuan" 王莽列傳
Wang Shenxu 王聖序
Wang Zijin 王子今
Wei 魏
*wei* 尉
"Wei Jiangjun Piaoqi liezhuan"

衛將軍驃騎列傳
Wendi 文帝
Wu Liang Shrine 武梁祠
Wudi 武帝
Wuding River 無定河
"Wudu fu" 吳都賦
Wushenqi 烏審旗
Wusun 烏孫
Wuyuan 五原
"Xi Qiang zhuan" 西羌傳
*xian* 仙
Xiayang 夏陽
Xihe (commandery) 西河(郡)
*Xijing zaji* 西京雜記
Xianyang 咸陽
"Xiao rong" 小戎
*Xiangrui* 祥瑞
Xiaotang shan 孝堂山
Xichagou 西岔溝
Xin Lixiang 信立祥
Xing Yitian 邢義田
Xinye 新野
Xiongnu 匈奴
"Xiongnu liezhuan" 匈奴列傳
Xiwangmu 西王母
Yanjiacha 延家岔
*yan she* 燕射
Yanjiacha 延家岔
Yangjingangcun 陽靳崗村
Yi 羿
"Yi jie" 猗嗟
*Yi li* 義禮
*Yilin yuekan* 藝林月刊
Yinan 沂南
Yin Mountains 陰山
Ying Shao 應劭
*yishe* 弋射
*"Yi Yi zhi Yi"* 以夷制夷
Yoshiko Doi 土居淑子
"Yüe ling" 月令
Yulin 榆林

Yunmeng 雲梦
*yunqi* 云气
Yu Xu 虞詡
Zeng Houyi 曾侯乙
Zhang Congjun 張從軍
Zhang Heng 張衡
Zhao (state) 趙
"Zhao hun" 招魂
"Zhu You Jing Dan Wang Liang Du Mao Ma Cheng Liu Long Fu Jun Jian Tan Ma Wu liezhuan"

朱景王杜馬劉傅堅馬列傳
"Zhui xing xun" 墜形訓
Zheng Xuan 鄭玄
*zhenmu wen* 鎮墓文
Zhongyang 中陽
*Zhou li* 周禮
Zizhou 子洲
Zuo Biao 左表
Zuo yu 驪虞
*Zuo Zhuan* 左轉